D0982523

OXFORD
ADDRESSES
ON POETRY

Robert Graves

OXFORD
ADDRESSES
ON POETRY

GREENWOOD PRESS, PUBLISHERS
NEW YORK   1968

Ad Coll. Sanct Joh. Bapt. Alumno
Cano Redeunti Benignissimum

First Greenwood reprinting, 1968

LIBRARY OF CONGRESS catalogue card number: 69-10102

PRINTED IN THE UNITED STATES OF AMERICA

Contents

Foreword

Last winter, after forty years of absence, most of them spent in a Majorcan mountain village, I was elected Professor of Poetry at Oxford, and welcomed home as something of a returned prodigal. Two or three revered Heads of Houses, the Merton Professor of English, and the Vice-Chancellor himself had, I found, been my fellow-undergraduates.

The Chair, founded in James I's reign, and not attached to any particular college, makes few demands on its occupants, apart from three annual lectures which I am allowed to concentrate in the Michaelmas term, thereby preserving my foreign domicile. Latin need no longer be used, and neither the subjects nor their treatment are limited by Statute.

The national press, to my regret, has misquoted me to the effect that Oxford knows nothing about poetry, and that sordid passion is a necessary part of a young poet's education. What I did say was that even at Oxford little is known about poetry except in the context of literary movements, and that *thwarted* passion stimulates poetic insight.

My public lectures ("public" meaning the University

public) discussed the hard core of our English poetic inheritance, namely poems inspired by the Muse rather than commissioned by Apollo, God of Reason. At Oxford a good many of the younger University members agreed with me that such poems are alone likely to survive concentrated pressure from commercialized or politically slanted literature and entertainment. The ornate academic Victorian tradition and the more recent but no less artificial Franco-American modernism, seemed to them equally bankrupt; and my strictures on Virgil were received without audible protest.

I include, for good measure, another three lectures given to University societies and all in some way concerned with my main theme. *The Word Báraka* had already served as the 1961 Blashfield Address to the American Academy and Institute of Arts and Letters at New York.

Deyá, Majorca, Spain.   R.G.

The Dedicated Poet

OXFORD CHAIR OF POETRY LECTURE I

I thank those of you members of Congregation who, last February, disregarded the warning of London's best-known literary weekly: to the effect that, though a poet, Mr. Graves could have nothing either novel or important to say from this Chair—which, it was added, might be better occupied by a Russian or French savant or, better still, by a bright young lecturer from a red-brick university. The same editorial insisted that the Professor you chose to address what would be predominantly an undergraduate audience, should adopt a serious moral attitude consonant with the dignity of his, or her, position. I do not dispute this last point; but poetic morals can surely be best discussed by poets, who, in the course of their labours, suffer pricks of professional conscience at which a Muscovite savant, or a bright young red-brick lecturer, cannot do more than guess.

This Chair, the only elective one at Oxford, has been linked by statute with the School of English Language and literature—albeit of far older foundation. The occupant is therefore expected to make no pronouncement irreconcilable with the view of poetry that tutors and examiners require from undergraduates. It may thus be

called a Siege Perilous: because Ben Jonson, of glorious
memory, to whom the young wits of Oxford used to flock
when in his old age he held forth at Great Tew, allowed
poets alone the faculty of judging poems; and few English
School tutors have been practising poets. . . . As Do-
mingo Ortega, the veteran bullfighter, remarked the other
day (the translation is mine):

> Bullfight critics ranked in rows
>   Crowd the enormous Plaza full;
> But only one is there who *knows*
>   And he's the man who fights the bull.

Of course, to be a practising poet is not necessarily to be a
good one. I know my own poetic limitations well enough,
and shall never forget the gentle rebuke once addressed
to me by a personal Muse:

> Forgive me, giver, if I destroy the gift!
> It is so nearly what would please me
> I cannot but perfect it.

Nevertheless, only a poet of experience can hope to put
himself in the shoes of his predecessors or contemporaries,
and judge their poems by re-creating technical and emotional dilemmas which they faced while at work on them.
The method may be called "analeptic mimesis": one slowly
copies out the poem by hand, as if it were a first draft of
one's own. When the pen checks at a word or a phrase,
one becomes intuitively aware of laziness, doubt, stupidity,
or some compromise with moral principle.

Yes: I know that Dr. Samuel Johnson sturdily rejected
Ben Jonson's view. He licensed non-poets to judge any
poem, on the ground that a man has a right to scold his
carpenter for making him a bad table. But this surely

begs the question? Granted that if Dr. Johnson bespoke a table, giving detailed instructions for its manufacture, he had every right to complain if these were disobeyed; but not since Sir Roger Newdigate founded his Prize, in the early nineteenth century, has it been seriously believed that even Universities have a right to bespeak poems. I am lucky, I confess. My Oxford English School colleagues still preserve the undogmatic and indulgent spirit I found displayed here soon after the First World War, when Sir Walter Raleigh was Merton Professor, and Mr. Percy Simpson my tutor. They neither encourage nor discourage undergraduates who choose to swim in the foul tidal basin of modernism: merely requiring from them a close attention to the primitive roots of our language and the long history of our literature. Yet this cannot be said of certain other English Schools. Besides, it is always tempting for tutors to commend the set Classics as worthy of a praise which few of them deserve —even if judged as literary fashion-plates, rather than as reading matter. And I have observed elsewhere that for most examinees the word "appreciate" has lost its original sense of "evaluation," and come to mean "admire."

The earliest and clearest example of the dedicated poet is John Skelton, one of Oxford's greatest glories, whom I discovered by accident in 1916, while on short leave from the Somme trenches; and on long leave from St. John's College. What heightened my shock of delight was that nobody else, it seemed, had felt as I did about him during the past four centuries.

Skelton, it is true, began his studies at Cambridge and probably took his B.A. there; but for a final academic polish came to "Oxforth" where, as he writes:

By whole consent of their Senáte
I was made Poet Laureate. . . .

This degree, taken in October 1488, according to Professor William Nelson, implied a diligent study of mediaeval grammar and rhetoric, though the *Poeta Laureatus* need not have written any poems—except perhaps a hundred Virgilian hexameters, and a Latin comedy, both eulogizing Oxford, to prove that he had mastered Latin prosody and the Aristotelian unities. Yet in old age, after being created *Orator Regius*, a sort of Latin Secretary, by his former pupil King Henry VIII, Skelton made a startling public avowal of devotion to the Muse-goddess, when he appeared wearing a white and green Court dress embroidered with the golden name CALLIOPE. He chose Calliope ("lovely face") rather than any of the Goddess's eight other names because, as he writes in an *amplificatio* of Diodorus Siculus' *History*, Calliope combines "incomparable riches of eloquence with profound sadness."

*Why Wear Ye "Calliope" Embroidered With Letters of Gold?
Skelton Laureate, Orator Regius, Maketh His Answer.*

> Calliope,
> As ye may see,
> Regent is she
>   Of poets all,
> Which gave to me
> The high degree
> Laureate to be
>   Of fame royál.
>
> Whose name enrolled
> With silk and gold
> I dare be bold
>   Thus for to wear

> Of her I hold,
> And her household.
> Though I wax old
>   And some-deal sere,
>
> Yet is she fain,
> Void of disdain,
> Me to retain
>   Her serviture:
> With her certáin
> I will remain
> As my sovereígn
>   Most of pleasure—
> *Maulgré touz malheureux.* . . .

He adds a *"latinum carmen,"* which I shall translate:

Calliope, who rules over prophetic poets, her white robe
embroidered with glittering gold, crowning Pierian devotees
with laurel: it is she whom I, a Pierian, shall ever account
worthy of the greatest honour while I still have life. And
though I grow old and my body slowly decays, yet I swear
still to wear this loyal pledge of her love, and yield to her
gentle poetic inspiration. Famous Calliope, whose image is
next to my heart! Thus speaks a Pierian, one more free than
any Spartan, since Calliope the most excellent, most beautiful, most shapely of the Muses, presides over my heroic
verses.

Historians will dismiss this as early Tudor rhodomon-
tade; but wrongly. "More free than any Spartan" gives
the clue. It refers to the famous stand of the Spartans at
Thermopylae, and Skelton is claiming as a poet the liberty
of thought and action which King Lycurgus' proto-Fascist
discipline denied even the most patriotic Spartans. (By
the way, they sent only a token force against the Persians
—300 out of the many thousands they could put into the
field.) Skelton explains in his play *Magnificence:*

To live under law it is captivity:
Where dread leadeth the dance there is no joy nor pride.
Or how can you prove there is felicity
An you have not your own free liberty
To sport at your pleasúre, to run and to ride?

He made good his claim to freedom by being the one man in England who, at the height of Cardinal Wolsey's power —when Dread led the dance—dared oppose him in cruelly satiric verses as a traitor to King, Church, and people. And though appointed Rector of Diss in Norfolk, by Royal favour, Skelton did not hesitate to take what was then called a "remedy" for his celibate condition—a regular concubine—with whom he lived until his death, and by whom he had several children. The following "Merry Tale of Skelton," a version which appeared while he was still alive, may well be authentic:

Skelton went into the pulpit to preach and said: "*Vos, estis, vos estis,*" that is to say: "You be, you be!" "And what be you?" said Skelton. "I say that you be a sort of knaves, yea and a man might say worse than knaves, and why I shall show ye. You have complained of me to the bishop that I do keep a fair wench in my house. I do tell you that if you had any fair wives, it were somewhat to help me at need. I am a man as you be. You have foul wives and I have a fair wench, of the which I have begotten a fair boy, as I do think, and as you all shall see."—"Thou wife," said Skelton, "that hast my child, be not afraid! Bring hither my child to me!" The which was done.
And he, showing his child naked to all the parish said: "How say ye, neighbours all? It hath nose, eyes, hands and feet as well as any of yours: it is not like a pig or a calf, nor like no fowl nor no monstrous beast. If I had," said Skelton, "brought forth this child without arms or legs or that it were deformed, being a monstrous thing, I would never have blamed you to have complained to the bishop of me. But to complain without a cause—I say, as I said before in my antethem, *vos estis,* you be,

and have been, and will and shall be, knaves, to complain of me
without a cause reasonable. . . . If that you exalt yourselves and
cannot be contented that I have my wench still, some of you shall
wear horns, and therefore *vos estis*, and so farewell!"

Nevertheless, Skelton's pledge to Calliope presumes his
knowledge of a different sort of love than the carnal
Remedy—the old solace which the parish of St. Ebbe's
used to offer Oxford Fellows under the ancient celibacy
rule; and this is evidenced by his *Divers Ditties Solacious*.
No more direct and sincere love poems had yet been
written in English. In his old age he called himself the
"British Catullus." The historic parallel is close, if only
because Catullus had dared satirize Julius Caesar at the
height of his power, and displayed the heart of a true
lover. Skelton writes with profound sadness to his un-
named Muse:

> Remorse have I of your most goodlihood,
>   Of your behaviour courteous and bening,
> Of your bountee and of your womanhood
>   Which maketh my heart oft to leap and spring
>   And to remember many a pretty thing;
> But absence, alas, with trembling fear and dread
> Abasheth me, albeit I have no need.
>
> You I assurë, absence is my foe,
>   My deadly woe, my painful heaviness.
> And if ye list to know the cause why so,
>   Open mine heart, behold my mind express! . . .
>   I would ye could! Then should ye see, maistress,
> How there nis thing that I covett so fain
> As to embrace you in my armës twain.
>
> Nothing earthly to me more désiróus
>   Than to behold your beauteous countenance.
> But, hateful Absence to me so envious,

Though thou withdraw me from her, by long distánce.
Yet shall she never out of rémembránce—
For I have gravèd her within the secret wall
Of my true heart, to love her best of all.

His *Garland of Laurell* addresses to a bevy of young
Court ladies, are well known. To Margery Wentworth:

With marjoram gentle
  The flower of goodlihood
Embroidered the mantle
  Is of your maidenhood. . . .

To Margaret Hussy:

Merry Margaret
A midsummer flower
Gentle as falcon
Or hawk of the tower. . . .

(By the way, he gets his own back on Mistress Gertrude
Statham, with whom he has had a tiff:

Though you were hard hearted
And I with you thwarted
With wordës that smarted. . . .

by wishing her the happy fate of Dame Pasiphaë—a
cruel mythological reference which she will certainly
have missed.)

Here I must distinguish, as I have done before, between
devotees of Apollo and those of the Muse. Apollonian
poetry is composed in the forepart of the mind: wittily,
should the occasion serve, always reasonably, always on
a preconceived plan, and derived from a close knowledge

of rhetoric, prosody, Classical example, and contemporary fashion. It may, of course, disguise simple statement in masquerade dress, but if so, observes all masquerade conventions; whether the dress chosen be mediaeval doublet and hose, pastoral smock, Roman toga, or pseudo-Homeric armour. The Apollonian allows no personal emotions to obtrude, and no unexpected incident to break the smooth musical flow of his verse. The pleasure he offers is consciously aesthetic.

Muse poetry is composed at the back of the mind: an unaccountable product of a trance in which the emotions of love, fear, anger, or grief are profoundly engaged, though at the same time powerfully disciplined; in which intuitive thought reigns supralogically, and personal rhythm subdues metre to its purposes. The effect on readers of Muse poetry, with its opposite poles of ecstasy and melancholia, is what the French call a *frisson*, and the Scots call a "grue"—meaning the shudder provoked by fearful or supernatural experiences.

If every Englishman were content to undergo a normal education, work hard in a regular job, order his life reasonably, marry a sensible woman, pay his taxes when required, be socially co-operative and count himself happy in such well-doing, then there would be little need for Muse poets. This sort of Englishman has never, as a matter of fact, been typical of our race. But since he is widely assumed as typical, it may be argued on his behalf: "Should we not esteem accomplished Apollonian poems above these products of morbid psychology? If the formal discipline of verse can endow a concept with grace and memorability, should we not regard loyal odes to the Sovereign, celebrations of rural pleasure, epic accounts of heroic feats, elegies for the dead, and stately epithalamia, as worthy of the highest honour?"

My answer is: No reason at all, if you have never felt a grue or *frisson* in your life, never fallen desperately in love, never faced personal disaster, never questioned the religious tenets of your childhood—no reason whatsoever, except perhaps this practical one; that the flowery age which bred such exercises is now long over-blown. Apollonian masterpieces may still arouse historic interest, but they have lost contemporary relevance—ask any librarian or publisher what demand there is for them, unless as required school or college text-books, or as morocco-bound prizes. To be honest: the refinement of quick, clean prose down the centuries, encouraged by cheap printing and universal literacy, and with it the provision of countless sharper, brighter pleasures than were ever before known, has made the formal Apollonian poem a dead bore to all but specialists. There is still room in modern life for the epigram, the topical squib, the *memoria technica*, the rhymed advertisement; but for what else? That a distinguished English bard has just published his autobiography in the form of a long blank-verse poem, does not weaken my contention: he is displaying once more his whimsical nostalgia for the irrecoverable past. But as the Apollonian poem fades away—despite bold attempts to revive its rhetoric by modernistic art-techniques borrowed from impressionism, expressionism, surrealism, or existentialism —so the Muse poem comes into its own.

Let me speak as a poet, rather than professor—in mythical language. An ancient Greek prophecy is being fulfilled before our eyes. Apollo, the god of Science, having formed a palace conspiracy with his half-brother Hermes, god of Politics, and his uncle Plutos, god of Money, has emas-

culated Almighty Zeus with the same curved sickle, laid up
at Sicilian Drepana, that Zeus used on his father Cronus.
Zeus still remains propped on his throne, but a Regency
Council of Three has taken over his powers. In this new
anarchical era anything may happen. That the Divine
Triumvirate are suspicious of one another, and that their
rival ambitions have made them careless of mankind, is
proved by the absurd cold war now being waged between
East and West, with the massive resources of Science,
Money, and Politics. They have cut civilization loose from
its moorings: familiar coasts of orthodox religion, philosophy, and economics fade in the dusky distance. Crazy
new cults are preached, old ones revived; ghosts sup-
posedly laid centuries ago creep out of their graves, not
only at dusk but by broad daylight. And the ancient
sovereign Goddess, who has been waiting these last three
thousand years to return with power, observes her op-
portunity. The political and economic emancipation of
women, which was needed to implement Zeus's downfall,
has had unforeseen consequences. Despite the successful
conversion of a great many of them, especially business
women and civil servants, not into matriarchs but into
pseudo-patriarchs, a small but powerful minority find
themselves free to be simply women, clear of male tutelage. With these newcomers woman's magical power over
man, so long curbed, reappears in something of its primitive glory and ferociousness; and the uglier the anarchy
caused by this demise of Father Zeus and the quarrels c⁵
his successors, the better become the Goddess' chances
of persuading mankind that she can offer a wholesome
change from the wholly negative cult of scientific pluto-
democracy. It is possible, of course, that the Triumvirate
will patch up their differences, make common cause, and

try to hang the Goddess from the vault of Heaven once
more, with anvils tied to her feet, which was Father Zeus's
way; or banish her to a nunnery, which was the Church
Fathers' way: but this can be no easy task. Meanwhile,
Muse-poets who understand what is happening, and what
is at stake, even more clearly perhaps than historians and
anthropologists, can provide the emotional physic to
which the rising generation, many of them painfully
caught in the Goddess' net, will take recourse. . . . I
hope I have not startled or offended you. My old friend
Max Beerbohm made an even direr prophecy in his
Zuleika Dobson: that of all young Oxford none but the
ignoble Noakes shall be proof against the Goddess' cruel
spell. . . . And that afterwards she will look up the trains
for Cambridge.

Back to Skelton, whose era was also one of change: the
Renaissance and the Breach with Rome having given the
Muse a foothold at Court, which she kept until dislodged
by Cromwell's Ironsides; and Skelton was her servant. It
is true that, as priest, scholar, and Court official, he could
not avoid writing ornate Apollonian verse in earnest of
his professional capacities—as Catullus had done—but he
did so with a covert half-smile at the understanding Muse.
For example, his *Prayer to the Father of Heaven:*

> O radiant Luminary of light intermináble,
>   Celestial Father, potential God of might,
> Of heaven and earth, O Lord incomparáble
>   Of all perfections the essential most perfite!
>   O Maker of Mankind, that formèd day and night
> Whose power imperial comprendeth every place—
>   Mine heart, my mind, my thought, my whole delight
> Is, after this life, to see thy glorious face.

Whose magnificence is incomprehensible,
  All arguments of reason which far doth exceed,
Whose Deity, doubtless, is indivisible,
  From whom all goodness and virtue doth proceed;
  Of Thy support all créatures have need.
Assist me, good Lord, and grant me of Thy grace
  To live to Thy pleasúre in wordë, thought and deed,
And, after this life, to see Thy glorious face.

Which leaves us dazzled, but cold; we even suspect that
Skelton has been naughtily ambiguous in his "*potential
God of might,*" and in "Whose Deity, *doubtless,* is indivis-
ible."

He also addressed the Second Person of the Trinity:

O bening Jesu, my sovereign Lord and King,
  The only Sonnë of God by filiation,
The Second Person, withouten béginning,
  Both God and man (our faith maketh relation)
  Mary, thy Mother, by way of incarnation—
Whose glorious passion our soulës doth revive
  Against all bodily and ghostly tribulation,
Defend me with thy piteous woundës five!

"Both God and man (our faith Maketh relation)": another
line of possible ambiguity. For Skelton had doubts about
the Real Presence, if we can believe the story of a palfrey
lent him by Bishop Stephen Gardiner. Instead of returning the beast as desired, Skelton sent the Bishop a verse
letter:

Non meministi
Quod mihi scripsisti
De corpore Christi?
Sic tibi rescribo
De tuo palfrido:
"Crede quod habes, et habes."

"You do not remember what you wrote to me about Christ's body. I write back the same thing about your palfrey: 'Believe that you have it, and you have it.'"

Yet when Skelton adopts an ancient sacrificial theme inspired by the Goddess, his lines are emotionally aflame:

> Woefully arrayed
> And shamefully betrayed.
>   My blood, man,
>   For thee ran,
> It may not be nayed:
>   My body blue and wan
> Woefully arrayed. . . .

> Thus naked am I nailèd, O man, for thy sake.
> I love thee, then love me. Why sleepest thou? Awake!
> Remember my tender heart root for thee brake,
> With painès my veinès constrainèd to crake.
>   Thus tuggèd to and fro,
>   Thus wrappèd all in woe,
>   Whereas never man was so
> Entreated thus in most cruel wise:
> Was like a lamb offered in sacrifice,
>   Woefully arrayed.

> Of sharp thorn I have worn a crown on my head,
> So painèd, so stainèd, so rueful, so red:
> Thus bobbèd, thus robbèd, thus for thy love dead,
> Unfainèd not deignèd my blood for to shed.
>   My feet and handès sore;
>   The sturdy nailès bore;
>   What might I suffer more
> Than I have done, O man, for thee?
> Come when thou list, welcome to me,
>   Woefully arrayed.

But the flame dies down again, and flickers out in ecclesiastic homily:

Dear brother, no other thing I of thee desire
But give me thine heart free to reward mine hire.
I wrought thee, I bought thee from eternal fire.
I pray thee, array thee toward my high empire
    Above the orient
    Whereof I am regent
    Lord God Omnipotent,
With me to reign in endless wealth.
Remember, man, thy soulës health.

To banish from his nostrils the odour of incense and
sweating Norfolk congregations, Skelton wrote *Philip
Sparow*. He used Goliardic verses, blithely parodying the
most sacred of Catholic Church rites: including the *Com-
mendatio Animae*, the *Officium Defunctorum*, the *Missa
pro Defunctis*, the *Absolutio super Tumulum*; and all in
honour of Jane Scroop's pet sparrow eaten by the Con-
vent cat at Carrow near Norwich. (It is, of course, an
elaboration of the *Passer mortuus est meae puellae* by
Catullus, whose *editio princeps* had been recently published.) Jane was not a little girl, as is often assumed, but
a beauty in her early twenties; and Skelton, the middle-
aged incumbent of nearby Diss, had fallen in love with
her. He makes Jane dwell on tender memories of Philip's
tricks and sports, and utter furious curses on the assassin:

Vengeance I ask and cry,
By way of exclamation,
On all the wholë nation
Of cats both wild and tame:
God send them sorrow and shame!
That cat especially
That slew most cruelly
My little pretty sparrow
That I brought up at Carrow. . . .

The léopards savàge,
The lions in their rage,
Might catch thee in their paws
And gnaw thee in their jaws;
The serpents of Libany
Might sting thee venomously;
The dragons with their tongues
Might poison thy liver and lungs;
The man-tigers of the mountains
Might feed them on thy brains . . .
Of Inde the greedy grypes
Might tear out all thy tripes;
Of Arcady the bears
Might pluck away thine ears;
The wild wolf Lycaon
Bite asunder thy back bone!
Of Etna the brenning hill
That day and night brenneth still
Set in thy tail a blaze
That all the world may gaze
And wonder upon thee,
From Ocean, the great sea,
Unto the Isles of Orcady,
From Tilbury Ferry
To the plain of Salisbury,
So traitorously my bird to kill
That never owed thee evil will. . . .

The humorous violence of this outburst is a measure of
Skelton's true feelings for Jane, whom he here boldly
deifies as the Muse herself! H. R. L. Edwards, a leading
authority on Skelton, emphasizes that in the passage en-
titled *Commendations*, which is a direct praise of Jane's
beauty, he has substituted *Domina* for *Domine* in all his
Biblical quotations. "Deal bounteously with thy servant,
that I may live, and my lips shall praise thee. Teach me,
Lady, the way of thy statutes. As the hart panteth for
the water brooks, so longeth my soul for thee, Lady. Re-

member thy word to thy servant—and I am thy servant."
(John Donne similarly substituted *Domina* for *Domine* in
a Biblical quotation written above an early portrait, discovered the other day, which shows him in a love-trance
"with folded arms and melancholy hat.") Skelton writes of
his Muse:

Her eyën grey and steep
Causeth my heart to leap,
With her browës bent
She well may represent
Fair Lucrece, as I ween,
Or else fair Polyxene . . .
Her beauty to augment
Dame Nature hath her lent
A wart upon her cheek
That seemeth from afar
Like to a radiant star—
All with favour fret
So properly is it set.
She is the violet,
The daisy délectable
The columbine cómmendáble
The jélofer ámiáble.
For this most goodly flour
This blossom of fresh colóur
(So Jupiter me secure)
She flourisheth new and new,
In beauty and virtúe,
Hac claritate gemina,
O gloriosa femina,
Bonitatem fecisti cum servo tuo, Domina,
Et ex praecordiis sonant praeconia.

"Thou hast dealt kindly with thy servant, Lady,
And from his heart rings out thy commendation."

Twenty years later, in his *Garland of Laurell* (1523),
Skelton finds himself obliged to defend *Philip Sparow*:

for although Jane originally asked him to write it, and although she fed his poetic flame, she now complains that he has insulted her—being by this time, alas, a respectable widow, relict of Thomas Brews, Esq., at whose side she lies on a funeral brass in the parish church of Little Wenham.

To know the Muse well, is to have experienced betrayal: the inevitable penalty of aspiring to her love. Skelton has not omitted to record this cruel aspect.

"My darling dear, my daisy flour,
    Let me," quoth he, "lie in your lap."
"Lie still," quoth she, "my paramour,
    Lie still, hardelý, and take a nap."
    His head was heavy, such was his hap,
All drowsy dreaming, drowned in sleep,
That of his love he took no keep,
    With "lullay, lullay, like a child
    Thou sleepst too long, thou art beguiled."

With "ba, ba, ba," and "bas, bas, bas,"
    She cherished him both cheek and chin,
That he wist never where he was;
    He had forgotten all deadly sin.
    He wanted wit her love to win.
He trusted her payment, and lost all his pay,
She left him sleeping, and stole away
    With "lullay lullay, like a child
    Thou sleepst too long, thou art beguiled."

The rivers rowth, the waters wan,
    She sparèd not to wet her feet;
She waded over, she found a man
    Who halsèd her hartly and kissed her sweet.
    Instead of a cold she caught an heat.
"My love," she said, "rowteth in his bed.
Ywis he hath an heavy head"—
    With "lullay lullay, like a child
    Thou sleepst too long, thou art beguiled."

What more natural than that Skelton should have earned the opprobrium of two prime English Apollonians, Milton and Pope? Milton, in his *Areopagitica*, even wanted Skelton's works censored! His outrageous low-life satire, *The Tunning of Elinour Rumming*, was the excuse for their attacks; but they clearly resented his earthy humour, reckless courage, poetic independence, and dedication to a personal Muse. No Apollonian dares lampoon a public figure of Cardinal Wolsey's stature, or parody Church ritual, or drink in country taverns with rogues and trollops, or publish scurrilous songs—nor does he wear CALLIOPE embroidered on his white and green Court dress. Though scorned as a mountebank, Skelton possessed higher scholarly distinctions than any of his traducers—degrees at Oxford, Cambridge (the only Laureate ever created there), and Louvain. The great Erasmus had hailed him in Latin verse as worthy of un-fading laurels, as inspired by Calliope, sweeter-throated than the dying swan, the rival of Orpheus himself. Britain (Erasmus insisted) should admit that her debt to Skelton equals that of Greece to Homer, Mantua to Virgil; for it was he who first introduced the Muses to his fellow-countrymen, who first taught them to speak their own language accurately and purely.

This is of course hyperbole. Skelton never claimed to be the father of English poetry, and acknowledged his filial affection for Chaucer, Gower, and Lydgate; though, as he rightly pointed out, "they lacked the laurel": the emblem of learning in the humanities. He was, however, not only the first scholar to write popular English verse, but the first Muse-poet to appear in England. (I am well aware that Chaucer toyed with the artificial French tradition of courtly love in his prologue to *The Legend of Good Women;* but long association with City merchants while Comptroller of Customs made a cynic of him. In *Troilus and Cresyde*, he plainly aligns himself with Pandarus, who persuades his niece that fine words butter no parsnips, and that she should take a practical view of her future.) A study of the *Oxford English Dictionary* will show that Skelton enriched our vocabulary more than any other poet before and since, even Chaucer. He also wrote the teasing, inconsequential, passionate *Speake Parot!*—its rolling stanzas liberally sprinkled with polyglot pseudo-learning, which Professor Ian Gordon calls the first modernist poem in England. Yet it is cut wholly from native cloth, in native fashion, and makes perfect sense to the informed reader—none of which things can be said of twentieth-century Anglo-American modernism.

In the bibliography attached to his *Garland of Laurell*, Skelton characteristically not only lists such Apollonian works as *The Book of Honorous Estate, The Book of the Rosary, Dialogues of Imagination*, his translations of Cicero's *Ad Familiares* and Diodorus Siculus' *History—* but interlards them with his wilder extravagances:

Of Mannerly Mistress Margery Milk and Ale,
  To her he wrote many matters of mirth,
Yet (though I say it) thereby lieth a tale:
  For Margery wincèd and brake her hinder girth.
  Lord, how she made muchè of her gentle birth!
With "Gingerly, go gingerly!" Her tail was made of hay;
Go she never so gingerly, her honesty's gone away.

The Duke of York's creauncer when Skelton was,
  Now Henry the Eighth, King of Engeland,
A treatise he devised and brought it to pass,

Called *Speculum Principis*, to bear in his hand,
Therein to readë, and to understand
All the demeanour of princely estate
To be our King, of God preordinate.

Also *The Tunning of Elinour Rumming*
With *Colin Clout, John Jew*, with *Joforth Jack*.
To make such trifles it asketh some cunning,
In honest mirth, pardee, requireth no lack;
The white appeareth the better for the black,
And after conveyance as the world goes
It is no folly to use the Welshman's hose.

"After conveyance as the world goes" means "since trickery is now in fashion"; "to use the Welshman's hose" means to take liberties with solemn texts—a Welshman's hose, like a shipman's hose, is one that will fit any leg.

The umbles of venison, the bottle of wine,
To fair Mistress Anne that should have been sent,
He wrote thereof full many a pretty line
Where it became, and whither it went,
And how that it was wantonly spent,
The Ballad also of the Mustard Tart—
Such problemës to paint, it 'longeth to this art.

Skelton could not repudiate the world unless perhaps by turning hermit like his saintly predecessor Richard Rolle of Hampole; and he enjoyed life too much for that. A dedicated poet is "a man as you be," who needs food, drink, lodging, and even domestic happiness—none of which benefits are bestowed on him without payment. But though he may make concessions to authority by wearing academic robes, or Court dress, or even a cassock, he must never smother poetic principle; must feel free to swap jokes with Mannerly Margery Milk and Ale,

John Jew, Joforth Jack, Elinour Rumming, and "Mistress Kate, that farley sweet, Who wones at the Key in Thamës Street."

Dedicated poets cannot exist in a vacuum, discarding all tradition, all knowledge, rejecting society. They must be at least as well grounded as was Shakespeare, whose Petty School *A.B.C. with the Catechism*, his *Primer and Catechism*, his *Book of Common Prayer* and *Psalter*, assisted him later to a self-education in more readable works. But Shakespeare was a special case; and so was John Clare, who had an equally limited schooling. I believe that every poet should read our English Classics, master the main grammatic rules before daring to bend or break them; should travel abroad, be at ease among all sorts and conditions of men, and experience not only the horrors of thwarted passion but, if he is fortunate, the tranquil love of an honest woman. The supreme gift bestowed on him by the Muse is that of poetic humour: a grasp of the identity of opposites, the wearing of Welshman's hose. Sometimes, in fact, when a poem has been assiduously refined and refined under the white blaze of inspiration, its final draft becomes so perfect in its ambivalence as to make the poet humorously doubt whether the insertion of a simple "not" will perhaps improve it.

Good manners demand that visitors should respect the laws of whatever society has courteously entertained them—court, university, public house, or gipsy camp; and poets, by their nature, are perpetual visitors. Skelton, like Naaman, bowed in the House of Rimmon, his fingers humorously crossed. I piously follow his example; and look with disgust on the so-called beatnik poets whose boast is that they conduct themselves with equal bad manners in all societies.

Erasmus referred to Skelton as a *vates*, and the inscription on Skelton's tomb at St. Margaret's, Westminster, ran: *Joannes Skelton, vates Pierius, hic situs est. Vates*, though occurring as a conveniently spondaic synonym for *poeta* in the *Gradus ad Parnassum*, means a good deal more than "poet." A *vates* is a prophet, one divinely possessed; one who must speak the truth, however strange or distasteful, and is sometimes granted visions both of the future and the past. *Pierian* means a native of Pieria, the district lying below Olympus, which was the birthplace not only of the poet Orpheus, but of the Ninefold Muse herself. The true Pierian limits his loyalties to those reconcilable with his worship of the Goddess "Whose service is perfect freedom"—a phrase, oddly enough, borrowed by St. Augustine from Apuleius' address to Isis, and by Thomas Cranmer from St. Augustine. The fewer the poet's affiliations, political, social, ecclesiastical, or scholastic, the better his chances of doing good work. Every gainful trade or profession has its characteristic occupational deformity: I have already mentioned Chaucer's Comptrollership of Customs. Shakespeare even regretted his actor-managership, complaining in a sonnet that the player's hand was dyed by it. And to avoid adopting a gainful trade or profession is difficult. Nevertheless, so long as a poet distinguishes Love from Remedy, and Wisdom from Learning; so long as he expects no rewards from the Muse nor any pity, never allows his business or domestic affairs to erase her name from the "secret wall of his true heart," never enlarges his public figure at the expense of his private self, the poetic trance may recur, from time to time, throughout his life. "Poor Devil" or "Lucky Devil"; it does not matter which you call him—the coin spins evenly.

Poets who decide to live by poetry, and remain otherwise uncommitted, should not understand "live by" in a financial sense. Until yesterday, or the day before, they were tempted to graduate as major poets—all Muse poetry is minor poetry, if length be the criterion—by writing verse plays or long philosophical works destined for posterity. Apollo would make them rich and famous, would secure them an honourable place in the curriculum —even name Ages after them. As I wrote once: "To invoke posterity is to weep on your own grave."

> And the punishment is fixed:
> To be found fully ancestral,
> To be cast in bronze for a city square,
> To dribble green in times of rain
> And stain the pedestal.

> Spiders in the spread beard;
> A life proverbial
> On clergy lips a-cackle;
> Eponymous institutes,
> Their luckless architecture.

> Two more dates of life and birth
> For the hour of special study
> From which all boys and girls of mettle
> Twice a week play truant
> And worn excuses try. . . .

Skelton pictures himself in *The Garland of Laurell* as conducted triumphantly to the Hall of Fame, where a whole crowd of authors—including such second-raters as Aulus Gellius, Sallust, Quinctilian, Quintus Curtius, Macrobius, Propertius, Poggio, and John Bochas—wait to greet him. Yet this is an elaborate joke against himself. Skelton knew just how good his writing was, and though he may have expected to live posthumously "where breath most breathes, even in the mouths of men" (a thought later borrowed by Shakespeare from Ennius), he cannot have been unaware that the mouths of men are highly unselective: filled with worthless tags from the least worthy of Apollonians—and even from anti-poets.

The Anti-Poet

OXFORD CHAIR OF POETRY LECTURE II

In my first address, a *captatio benevolential* suitable to the occasion, I spoke about the dedicated Muse poet, taking John Skelton as my chief example. Today, secure I hope in this captured benevolence, I shall deal with the Apollonian anti-poet, his precise opposite; and though this will break an eight-hundred-year-old academic tradition at Oxford, my example must be Publius Vergilius Maro, *alias* Virgil, who has for two thousand years exercised an influence over Western culture out of all proportion to his merits either as a human being or as a poet. Virgil's pliability; his subservience; his narrowness; his denial of that stubborn imaginative freedom that the true poets who preceded him had valued; his perfect lack of originality, courage, humour, or even animal spirits—these were the negative qualities which first commended him to government circles, and have kept him in public favour ever since.

A brief biography. Virgil was born (70 B.C.) at Andes, a marshland village near Mantua, in Transpadine Gaul. Although of military age when Julius Caesar's legions crossed the Rubicon and swept through the province, this dark-complexioned, heavily-built man never bore arms either for or against Caesar: a weak digestion, a delicate

throat, bleeding piles and frequent headaches offered suf-
ficient excuse. He avoided the loud, obscene tavern talk of
military friends, and his girlish shyness presently earned
him the nickname "Parthenias" ("the maiden"). Virgil's
father, a bee-keeper and hired man to a magistrate's clerk,
had succeeded in marrying the clerk's daughter; which
helped him to improve his property by buying up wood-
lands and selling the timber.

Virgil attended school at near-by Cremona, and there
discovered a facility for versification. Beginning on epi-
grams, he was soon penning narrative pieces of some
length. From Cremona the proud family sent him to
Milan; thence to Naples, where he studied Greek, the
language of higher education; and finally to Rome, where
he completed his rhetorical studies under the best available
professor: Syron the Epicurean. If Virgil's Greek was
rather poor, as his occasional misrenderings of Homer
prove, this must be pardoned him: a course at Athens
would have been beyond the family's means—and Oxford
still lay in the womb of Time.

Two centuries before, Greek rhetoric and poetry had
been imported to Rome and, by Virgil's day, young
Roman noblemen usually travelled abroad to study.
Though more attracted to rhetoric, as a means of political
advancement, than to poetry, they could not avoid the
required course in Poetics, which meant learning by heart
as much as possible of Homer's *Iliad* and *Odyssey*. They
thus became aware of the strict Greek laws governing
scansion. Their own native Saturnian metre, as handled
by Naevius, the father of Latin poetry, enjoyed so much
rhythmic freedom that it now looked barbarous to them
—like the old Roman habit of building temples by eye,

not by the rules of geometry, mensuration and the Golden
Section. They could hardly point to a single "normal" line
in all Naevius, whose scansion was accentual as opposed
to quantitative. That is: instead of depending, as Homer
did, on the calculated length of each syllable (doomed to
be either short or long), and allowing so many short or
long syllables to each foot, Naevius depended on the
natural stresses of speech—as in English ballad poetry.
That the same word could be accentuated differently in
different parts of the same poem, changing from short to
long and back again according to stress, seemed arbitrary
and illogical to these Roman students.

They shamefacedly renounced their natural ballad inheritance and went all Greek. Naevius found no literary
successors. Depressed by the encroachment of Greek and
a gradual falling-off in the standard of pure colloquial
Latin, he had written his own epitaph, as a slow march:

> Mortales immortales
> Flere si foret fas,
> Flerent divae Caménae
> Naevium poetam.

Itaque:

> Postquam est Orcino
> Traditus thesauro
> Obliti sunt Romae
> Loquier Latina lingua.

which means:

> Were deathless gods permitted
> Weeping for dead mortals,
> Each Muse divine would weep for
> Naevius, her poet.

And so:

> Since to Hell's own storehouse
> He has been committed,
> Rome is grown forgetful
> Of her native Latin language.

Ennius, the first Roman (so far as I know) to experiment with a quantitative hexameter, became the step-
father of Latin poetry; educating it by sternly suppressing
its natural inclinations. The results will, at first, have
sounded as comic as those English ones which Edmund
Spenser composed:

Nōble Alēxāndēr//when he cāme to the tōmb of Achīllēs
Sīghing spāke with a bīg//voīce ō thrīce blēssèd Achīllēs
Thāt such a trūmp, sō grēat//sō loūd sō glōrious hāst foūnd
Aō the renōwnēd ānd, sūrprīsīng ārch-poet Hōmer!

Fortunately, the attempt to force English poetry into a
Classical strait-jacket failed. George Chapman wrote, in
his *Shadow of Night:*

>   . . . Sweet poesy
> Will not be clad, in her supremacy
> With those strange garments (Rome's hexameters)
> As she is English; but in right prefers
> Our native robes (put on with skilful hands—
> English heroics) to those antique garlands.

In establishing his new metre, Ennius had to create a
special poetic vocabulary of dialect or obsolete forms to
assist versification. His trouble was that a number of Latin
words were excluded by their scansion from the hexameter. I have elsewhere instanced the famous Roman
name Domitius Ahenobarbus. "Domitius" contains four
short syllables in a row, and "Ahenobarbus" has a short

syllable hopelessly imprisoned between two long ones. So
if one wished to write the hexameter: "And Domitius
Ahenobarbus also came," the only way out would be to
address him in the vocative—*Domiti*—which is a manageable word; and to use the historical present for "came";
and to explain "Ahenobarbus" as meaning "Brazen
Beard":

Tū-que venīs, Domitī, quēm sīgnat ahēnea bārba . . .

(And thou comest also, Domitius, whom a brazen
beard distinguishes.)

And because the word *āudiūnt* ("they hear") cannot be
used in a hexameter, third persons plural must always "per-
ceive with their ears," instead of simply "hearing," or use
the past tense.

Virgil employed numerous other tricks and evasions for
supplying manageable words. Also, as I shall show, he
further divorced poetry from common sense by the ex-
ploitation of "poetic licence." An "olde worlde" vocabulary, unnatural grammatic inversions, and poetic licence
were among the many curses bequeathed to English Apollonian poetry by the Virgil cult. Nevertheless Latin accentual verse remained fixed in popular song—the Legions
used it—and eventually triumphed in such sacred chants
as *Dies irae, Dies illa* and in drinking songs like *Mihi est
propositum* in *taberna mori.*

Virgil's four principal predecessors, the poets Naevius,
Ennius, Lucretius and Catullus, were men of determina-
tion, and had something urgent to say. Naevius, a First
Punic War veteran, satirized the haughty Metellians who
then dominated Rome, and served a prison sentence for
it. Ennius fought as an infantry captain in Sicily and re-

engaged for the Aetolian campaign; his surviving verse fragments show a tough spirit and imaginative magnificence. A gap of more than a century separated Ennius from Virgil's elder contemporaries Lucretius and Catullus.

Lucretius, a forthright Calabrian provincial, used Ennian hexameters, now at last naturalized, for preaching scientific godlessness to the religious-minded Romans. Since he chose a most difficult theme, *The Nature of Things*, and since Latin was still singularly barren of abstract words, he faced linguistic problems that had not troubled Ennius; but his passion often broke through the philosophic argument in lines of unmistakable beauty.

Catullus, a young Veronese nobleman, had learned from the Alexandrian critics that all long poems have their boring passages, and that to bore is the worst crime a poet can commit. He therefore wrote no epics, constantly varied his metres, and did not let metrical difficulties thwart the plain sense of a poem by driving him to clever periphrasis. Catullus lived a violent, gay life at Rome, often running into debt, and expressed his loves, hates, griefs and bawdy humour with absolute freedom. While admiring Julius Caesar, he dared publish two most offensive lampoons on him.

The timorous, inoffensive Virgil, in contrast, found so little to say of personal value that the themes of both his best-known poems, *The Georgics* and *The Aeneid*, were forced on him by patrons. He never lampooned those in power, and never got into scrapes. He bartered his talent for social security; and wrote only hexameters—to which, for the sake of elegance, he applied new constrictive rules. Nor did he ever invent where he could borrow. Quintus Octavius Avitus later published an eight-volume collection of Virgil's plagiarisms—sources and all—but this ranked as no demerit in official quarters, so long as the sources were Greek classics. And when accused of filching from Homer, Virgil replied disarmingly: "Why don't my critics try to follow my example? They will find it no easier than to steal Hercules' club." He had also plagiarized Latin contemporaries, including Parthenius, his old Bithynian schoolmaster; for no Roman copyright laws restrained him.

Thus, further evil bequests of Virgil's have been the notions that borrowing from the classics proves a poet's modesty and good sense; and that style is more important than subject. And, though verse epics have ceased to be fashionable, clever poets of the Establishment are still Virgilian enough to conceal recondite Classical beauties in their works, for the well-read reader to greet with self-satisfied smirks.

To resume the brief biography. One of Virgil's early poems, *The Gnat*, has survived. This is the plot: a certain shepherd falls asleep and is warned of a poisonous snake approaching him by a gnat, which impulsively stings his forehead. He flattens the gnat with a blow of his fist, and by good luck kills the snake at the same time. Then he builds the gnat a tomb, inscribing on it this touching epitaph:

> Poor little gnat, well-deserving! The guardian shepherd
>   now offers,
> Grateful for this kind gift, due funeral rites at your
>   tombstone.

Dissatisfied with such trifling, Virgil felt called upon to versify Roman history; perhaps because in 49 B.C., when he was twenty years old, a decree had given full Roman citizenship to all towns of the province.

Five years later, a fortunate accident launched him into fame. His family were threatened with forcible eviction from the farm at Andes by discharged veterans of Caesar's —they were planting a colony between Cremona and Mantua. The story can be read in Virgil's *Eclogues*, which are drawing-room pastorals based on the *Idylls* of Theocritus. First, he appeals for help to the poet Cornelius Gallus, who has studied beside him at Rome under Syron; and Gallus, now one of the triumvirate who have distributed land among these veterans, recommends Virgil to Asinius Pollio, the bookish Provincial Governor. "Ah, so you are a poet, too, my dear fellow?" we can hear Pollio saying. "Our common acquaintance Gallus mentions your talent, in this note. Let me see if it will justify our intervention!" Virgil hands Pollio his patriotic verses. They pass muster, and Virgil's plea is granted.

We next find him admitted to Pollio's *salon* and dutifully applauding his tragedies, though so dry-as-dust an orator can hardly have been much livelier as a poet. Virgil stood on the same easy terms with Gallus. Times had changed. The noble Scipio Africanus, who supported Polybius the historian and Terence the playwright, kept these gifted commoners at a certain distance. But when Julius Caesar broke social conventions, choosing his friends for their usefulness to him, not for their birth, all barriers were down. Gallus himself was a "New Man," the grandson of an emancipated slave from Fréjus.

Pollio's command passes to Alfenus Varus (whom commentators have confused with one Atius Varus, and make a former fellow-student of Virgil's), and Virgil hears that the farm is threatened again. He appeals for Varus' help,

in an eclogue; but Varus replies that he can do nothing.
Gallus then investigates the case on Virgil's behalf, accuses a local magistrate at Cremona of allowing veterans
to occupy lands not mentioned in the grant, and sends
Virgil with his plea directly to the Supreme Court; where
Augustus decides in his favour. Virgil's eclogue of acknowledgment proffers Augustus divine honours. Later,
Varus brazenly asks Virgil to make good a promise that,
if he regains the property, "vocal swans shall bear thy
name, Varus, to the skies!" The matter has now been arranged, Varus says, so will Virgil please celebrate his
military exploits? Not wishing to offend Pollio and Gallus by flattering the unhelpful Varus at their expense, or
to offend Varus by a direct refusal, Virgil borrows a
polite formula of evasion from the Alexandrian poet Cal-
limachus. He is at present writing only pastorals, he says,
"having ceased to sing of wars and kings." And a shepherd,
though he may feed his flock until they are fat, slow and
heavy, must not let the same thing happen to his poems—
by adopting the heroic style. However, he adds, Varus
will find numerous poets eager to undertake this worthy
task.

One eclogue condoles with Gallus on the loss of his
beloved mistress, a stage singer. Commentators inform us
that she was Lycoris, in whose praise Gallus had written
a whole volume of elegiac poems, and that she deserted
him for the protection of Mark Antony, Augustus'
powerful colleague and rival. Since, according to Suetonius' *Life of Virgil*, Virgil's *Eclogues* were stage suc-
cesses, it has been plausibly suggested that Lycoris sang
them. And that the provincials in applauding her were
applauding her protector—and their own.

In another piece, Virgil sympathizes with the middle-aged Pollio for having failed to seduce a handsome boy. It was genuine sympathy, not toad-eating, because (Suetonius reports) Virgil himself suffered from pederastic passion. His particular favourite was an educated slave, afterwards given him by Pollio, whom he has celebrated in an eclogue as "Daphnis"; and his second favourite was young Cebes—another slave, but a poet in his own right.

Virgil encourages Pollio's perversion and applauds his tragedies. Probably he reads them aloud—"the poet Montanus," Suetonius remarks, "used to declare that verses which convinced the audience when Virgil read them with his beautiful voice, wonderful facial expression, and dramatic power, sounded flat and toneless from another's lips." We also learn that when Lucius Varus, the poet, tried to cure Virgil of his inveterate homosexuality by arranging for him to get into bed with one Plotia Hieria, he shrank from the ordeal horror-stricken.

This takes us, in our worldly wisdom, a little further. It has long been a habit of actresses and high-class courtesans to choose gentle, lonely half-men as their confidantes, and we may suppose that Gallus, when busy at his magistrate's court or army headquarters, engaged Virgil to act as Lycoris' escort. A practical argument against heterosexual passion and rough male brawling occurs in his *Fourth Georgic:*

But nothing so strengthens the power of a male animal, whether stallion or bull, as to restrain him from desire. A bull is therefore banished to lonely pastures beyond a hill or river; for the sight of a female slowly wastes his strength and, what is more, she often drives her proud lovers to settle their differences with clash of horns.

Virgil's fear of destructive females explains Juno, Aeneas'
persecutrix in the *Aeneid;* also the savage vilification of
Cleopatra, Mark Antony's seductress; and Aeneas' scarcely
controlled impulse to butcher Helen of Troy.

Virgil spent three years on the *Eclogues,* before climb-
ing into an even higher social sphere. He secured the
patronage of Maecenas, Minister of Literature, Propaganda, and the Fine Arts, who had been Gallus' contact at
Court when Virgil took his plea there. In 39 B.C., Maecenas, though admiring the elegance of the *Eclogues,*
asked Virgil to write on a less trivial theme. Unwilling to
risk his neck by attempting political projects—the quarrel
between Augustus and Mark Antony was still undecided
—Virgil compromised by agreeing, instead, to write a long
poem in aid of agriculture. "Very well, my friend," says
Maecenas, "you have proved yourself the Latin Theocritus.
Now become the Latin Hesiod! Write Georgics."

Virgil had left the farm at too early an age to have
acquired any practical knowledge of agriculture; and
Hesiod, a sour, pessimistic, litigious Greek peasant who
believed, like the author of *Genesis,* that God had invented
work as a curse upon mankind, was no soul-mate of
Virgil's. Moreover, Hesiod's *Work and Days* provided
material for only the First Book of *Georgics.* He stuck at
this point until, two years later, by good fortune, the
famous Roman know-all Varro began to publish a *Treatise on Agriculture.* Virgil then quarried from Varro, and
from Cato's *Rustic Economy.* Though having also collected such copious Greek reference works as Aristotle's
Zoology, Nicander's *Bestiary,* Theophrastus' *Botony,* and
Eratosthenes' *Astronomy,* he found his task heavy enough
going, and took seven years to finish it—at the average

rate of one line a day. Even so, I suspect that clever little Cebes drafted plenty of them.

Nobody (except Virgil himself, in a suppressed but extant foreword to the *Aeneid*) has ever called the *Georgics* a "useful work for farmers." They come little closer to real life than the *Eclogues*. Seneca observes: "His aim is not truth but beauty; not agricultural information but literary pleasure." Guided by Virgil, the Roman city-dweller could dream about simple rural joys, and feel himself at one with his farming ancestors—even if he had never in his existence handled a hoe, milked a goat, or tended more than an ornamental window-box. This waiving of factual truth has since become fixed in the popular imagination as "poetic"; and few poets have escaped the taint.

An obstinate late-Victorian tradition praises the *Georgics* for upholding the "dignity of labour," for expressing "a devotion to Rome founded on local devotion to a particular region, village, family, farm," and for reminding absentee landlords of their duty to the soil. But no modern historian can accept Virgil's picture of stout Roman yeomen ploughing ancestral acres, secure in their title-deeds, proud of gnarled parents and sturdy sons, offering pious sacrifices to old-fashioned rustic gods. "Peasants are not tempted by luxury," Virgil claims. "Justice reigns among them, and the daily round perfects their morals." A more honest poet would have anticipated Goldsmith's *Deserted Village*, in distress that Augustus' victories had dealt another heavy blow to traditional Italian agriculture by further encouraging the growth of large estates run on slave labour. Smallholders could no longer compete against the low prices at which estate owners marketed their produce. They must sell out and join the

dole-collecting city rabble, or starve, or find employment
as estate foremen.

"Labour conquers all!" exults Virgil, using "labour" in
its most idealistic sense. Yet when he himself grew weary
of Rome's noise and bustle, did he return to the family
farm at Andes and sacrifice unblemished lambs of his own
raising to Pales, Faunus and Picus? Indeed, no! He bought
a slave-run estate at fashionable Nola, Augustus' birthplace. . . . The polished *Georgics* make simple, quaint
reading where Virgil has versified the works of Cato or
Varro; but here is his address to the sturdy yeomen whom
he has just been lecturing on cattle-raising:

> Sed fugit interea, fugit inreparabile tempus . . .

> But time meanwhile is flying, flying beyond recall, while
> we, charmed with love of our theme, linger around each
> detail! Enough, now, for the herds; there remains the second
> part of my task, namely to describe the tending of fleecy
> flocks and shaggy goats. In this theme lies labour, hence
> hope of fame, my sturdy yeomen! And though well I know
> how hard it is for me to win a triumph here by crowning
> a lowly theme with glory, yet sweet ambition hurries me up
> the lonely steeps of Parnassus. How joyful it is to roam over
> heights where no forerunner's track slopes gently down to
> the Castalian spring . . .

As if the struggling peasant would care a sesterce what
fame this patronizing city-man earned!

Virgil continues his lecture:

> First, then, I decree that [when winter hardens] your
> sheep shall crop the herbage in soft pens, till leafy summer
> soon returns, and that you strew the hard ground beneath
> them with straw and handfuls of fern, lest the chill ice harm
> the tender flock, bringing scab and unsightly foot-rot . . .

The omissions from the *Georgics* are significant of complete disinterest in Virgil's ostensible theme. For example, when Varro's *Treatise on Agriculture* gives advice on the care of asses, pigs, and hens, Virgil hurriedly turns the page: Maecenas will not consider such topics idyllic enough. Instead, he goes elsewhere to borrow a fine purple passage about race horses, which should please the Roman Hippodrome audience—although well aware that horses formed no part of peasant economy.

Augustus, returning in triumph from Actium, paused at Atella to cure an infected throat, and there Virgil read the *Georgics* to him on four successive days, Maecenas taking over whenever Virgil grew hoarse or faint. Since four days of this monotonous entertainment seems a long time for a busy man to endure, we must suppose his interest to have been neither poetic nor agricultural. Rather, he was pondering Maecenas' view that Latin literature could at last challenge Greek in all fields, except the Homeric corpus of epic poetry, and that this field must likewise be conquered. Virgil, already Rome's Theocritus, had now improved on Hesiod, and would be just the man to write the official Roman epic, glorifying the divinely-descended Caesars as fated rulers of the world. The *Georgics* brought Augustus over to Maecenas' view; and Virgil hitherto reluctant to "sing of wars and kings" and "to feed his sheep until fat, slow and heavy," dared not flout the sacred wish. He accepted the *Aeneid* commission, though plainly finding this a most uncongenial task.

"Make it a mirror of both the *Iliad* and the *Odyssey*," says Maecenas. "You can draw heavily on those two, and on our own poetical history—Aeneas' visit to Dido, for example, has been celebrated by Naevius and Ennius— and on the historians Dionysius, Hellanicus, Timaeus, Cato

and Varro. I can lend you the scrolls. But in describing
Aeneas' struggle against the natives of Italy, try to give
no offence: foreshadow the present era when every Italian is proud to call himself a Roman. Meanwhile, the
Emperor will maintain you worthily. How would you
like a house on the Esquiline Hill, near my gardens?
. . . I trust you to sound the correct note: an appeal for
national unity, peace and hard work under the aegis of
Augustus Caesar, incarnate God of Success!"

Thereupon, so Suetonius tells us, Virgil drafted a prose
version of the *Aeneid*, which he slowly turned into verse:
dodging from book to book, as the fancy took him. He
chose the easiest options first. Four years afterwards
(27 B.C.) Augustus wrote from Spain demanding extracts,
but Virgil excused himself: no book was ready, he an-
swered, and he felt a fool to have undertaken so ambitious
a work, especially when faced with the arduous commission of modelling his epic on far more distinguished ones.
He did not mention other troubles: that ancient Roman
history was a hopeless jumble of irreconcilabilities, and
that he found it hard to hit upon a legend decently eulogizing Augustus' ancestor Aeneas—who, the mythographers agreed, had betrayed his overlord King Priam,
and sold Troy to the Greeks at the price of a safe-conduct
through their lines.

In 24 B.C., the poet Propertius gave the *Aeneid* advance
publicity:

Yield, Roman writers; yield, you Greeks; for now
A greater than the *Iliad* has been born!

And, by the seventh year, Virgil had (like a she-bear with
her cub—his own expression) licked the Second, Fourth

and Sixth Books into a fairly presentable shape, and read
them to Augustus. Those later books about the wars in
Italy must have been a dreary assignment; but he could
not avoid it. Ignorant of soldiering, he flavoured passages
from Roman legend with imitations from the *Iliad*, the
Odyssey, and Apollonius' *Argonautica*. In the *Iliad*,
Achilles' horses shed tears when Patroclus dies, so in the
Aeneid Pallas' team do the same; and the god Hephaestus
forges picturesque arms for Achilles, so the god Vulcan
forges even better ones for Aeneas. Virgil's chief delight
was to mourn beautiful boys cut off in the flower of their
youth—ah, what a waste!

> Euryalus rolls over in death. Athwart his lovely limbs
> runs the blood—and his drooping neck sinks on his shoulder.
> As when a purple flower lopped by the plough-share droops
> in death, or as when poppies with weary neck bow the head
> when weighted by some chance shower . . .

I find this much-admired passage poetically inept. Poetry
must be practical. Once blood has suffused Euryalus'
limbs, the purple or scarlet colour of the flower should
not be stressed; after all, Euryalus' head was uninjured,
and would have grown pallid in comparison with his
bloody limbs. Also, the simile is false: when the root of
a plant has been sliced by a plough-share, its flower gradually droops; a lopped flower, however, has no chance to
do so. The alternative simile of the poppy weighted
down by rain comes straight from the *Iliad*, but Virgil
spoils it, changing "poppy" to "poppies," which scan
better. (How hard to filch from Homer!)

Virgil's handling of the Dido and Aeneas episode re-
veals his character. When Aeneas' fleet reaches Carthage,
Queen Dido and he fall in love with each other. But this is

a mere stratagem arranged by the Goddess Venus, his mother, to protect the Trojan refugees from massacre; and Aeneas is willing to desert Dido as soon as high destiny orders a resumption of his interrupted voyage. Dido utters a passionate plea for him to stay. Aeneas answers (to quote my old schoolmaster, Mr. T. E. Page) "with the cold and formal rhetoric of an attorney." Dido, after another hysterical outburst, sinks distraught into her attendants' arms. Aeneas, stammering and "ready to say a great deal more," makes a disgusted exit. T. E. Page indignantly describes the next paragraph, which begins: "*But the good Aeneas* . . ." as one of the puzzles of literature.

I cannot agree. Women, except comfortable kindly matrons (Venus always appears to Virgil in maternal, never in erotic, guise) or sexless Amazons like the Italian heroine Camilla, left him cold; hysterics frightened him. But here is a real puzzle of literature: Aeneas' son Ascanius, when bribing Nisus to undertake a raid, promises him not twelve beautiful captive princesses skilled in all the arts, as in the *Iliad*, but "twelve captive mothers!" What on earth would Nisus want with twelve? Men of Virgil's temperament notoriously welcome a broad black-satin bosom to sob upon; yet surely *one* captive mother would have sufficed?

Commenting on the scene where Aeneas subsequently meets Dido in Hell, one of our senior literary church-wardens has written:

Virgil excuses himself: "I was under the God's orders," he says. "I didn't want to do it. I am sorry you took it so hard." Dido avoids his gaze and turns away, with a face like flint. I have no doubt that Virgil when he wrote these lines, was assuming the rôle of Aeneas and feeling decidedly a worm.

Yet anyone who reads the passage carefully, will see that Aeneas, so far from feeling a worm, was spitefully getting his own back on Dido. He found her in the close, if shadowy, embrace of her former husband Sychaeus (or Sicharbas), who remained as yet unaware that she had injured his memory by a crazy love affair. Aeneas, a cad to the last, insults them both by bringing up the shameful adventure under cover of an apology. What is more, we learn from Justin, Servius, and Silius Italicus that Virgil is grossly libelling womankind. The original Punic legend makes Dido pursued in her widowhood by the Libyan prince Hiarbas, who offers her the choice of marriage or death. She sacrifices victims to the shade of her husband, and bravely leaps on her own funeral pyre. St. Jerome comments drily: "St. Paul thought it better to marry than to burn; Dido disagreed."

Conticuere omnes, intenti-que ora tenebant . . .

(They kept silence and, being attentive, held their mouths.)

This hexameter, which opens Book Two, was the first line of the *Aeneid* that Augustus heard Virgil recite. Reading it again, after a lapse of fifty years, I seemed to be back at Charterhouse, teasing gentle old Tommy Page, the Sixth Form Beak: "*Who* all kept silent, sir? And why write the same thing in two different ways? . . . Yes, sir, I know—the *notes* say that 'all' means Dido's courtiers; but why doesn't Virgil?"

Tommy replies: "You suggest, my boy, that he might have written straight out:

Intenti comites Didonis conticuerunt . . .

(Dido's courtiers preserved an attentive silence.)

"Well, Virgil, as it happens, thought that Lucretius and Homer, who did not mind ending a hexameter line with a single, five-syllabled verb, were inelegant; so *conticuerunt* had to begin the line and take the poetic form of *conticuere*. That suggested *omnes* as a means of removing the final 'e' by elision—*conticuer' omnes*. Virgil's readers could be allowed to guess at the meaning of *omnes*, in return for the elegant trope, borrowed perhaps from the Orient, and often miscalled *hendiadys*, of saying the same thing, differently, twice over. He uses it several times, you'll have noticed, when telling us about the Wooden Horse. The Greeks 'enclose chosen bodies of men in the sides of the horse' *and fill the mighty central cavern with armed soldiers.* When they have sailed away, the Trojans 'find the Greek camp deserted' *and the shore abandoned.* Thymoetes then orders the Trojans to push into the sea 'the wiles of the Greeks' *and the gifts they suspected* (but that's true *hendiadys*, not repetition); whereupon Laocoon hurls his spear 'into the side' *and the carved flank* of the animal; as a result of which *the stomach being struck,* its 'hollow interior makes a sound' *and the caverns groan.*"

"Thank you, sir! Another thing we can't make out is what wood the Trojan Horse was really built of."

"Fir, my boy. Line 16."

"Yes, sir, it's fir in line 16, but it's maple in line 112, and oak in line 186, and pine in line 258, and oak again in line 280 . . ."

"Yes, now I remember. But in Virgil's time a poet was licenced to use any particular sort of timber as a synonym for timber generally, even if it involved him, as here, in apparent contradictions."

"Thank you again, sir!"

The child has been father to the man. My adult eye is offended by numerous other examples of poetic bad manners in the same passage, such as the verse-endings *sanguine cretus* and *cum sanguine poscunt* occurring close together, although *sanguine* means "lineage" in the first case, and "bloodshed" in the second—a similarity without relevance. And *fatur* ending one line, and *fatebor* the next; again a similarity without relevance. And three ugly lines all appearing on the same page:

Illi me comit[em] et: consanguinitate propinquum . . .

Promis[i]ultor[em] et: verbis odi[a] aspera movi . . .

Hoc Ithacus velit et: magno mercentur Atridae . . .

The English equivalent would be:

Me as his tent-fellow *and* related to him by a blood-tie . . .

Vengeance I promised him *and* caused hate by my eloquent roughness . . .

Pleasing the Ithacan, *and* the Atreidae would handsomely pay you . . .

Homer, when he willed this stately measure, never left an *and* suspended in the air at the end of his half-line!

Also I come across such meaningless, if elegant, rhetoric as:

> . . . jam nox umida caelo

Praecipitat, suadent-que cadentia sidera somnos.

(Now damp night precipitates itself from the sky, and the descending starts encourage sleep.)

"Damp night" probably refers to dew; but does the word *praecipitat* mean that night is falling (as we English say)?

Or does it, as in Cicero and Ovid, mean that night is drawing to a close? The context will not help us, neither will "descending stars": because all night long some stars dip towards the Eastern horizon, just as all night long others rise from the West. But the *Homeristae* had, for centuries, made a profession of commenting on Homeric problems, and now *Virgilistae* were herewith invited to a fresh banquet of commentary.

When Virgil died at the age of fifty-one, worth something like a quarter of a million pounds in modern money, the *Aeneid* was complete but not yet published. Conscious of its defects, and perhaps even (let us be fair to him) repentant, he asked his executors to burn the manuscript. Augustus, of course, would not permit that. Having invested heavily in the production, he ordered it to be published without delay. Rome chorused approval, and soon Caecilius Epirota had fixed Virgil in the Latin school curriculum, where he has remained ever since. The one discordant note was struck by tough old Vipsanius Agrippa, who had not only won the Battle of Actium for Augustus, but settled the Spanish War, restored peace to Gaul, overawed Pontus, and conciliated the Jews. He said bluntly: "Virgil, a poet first foisted on us by Maecenas, has invented a new bad way of imitating the classics. Neither bombastic nor dry, he employs a restrained poetic vocabulary, which makes his failings less obvious."

Anchises' prophecy in the Sixth Book beginning *Excudent alii*, a favourite declamation of imperialists who consider themselves heirs of Augustan Rome, awards the Greeks credit for greater eloquence than the Romans in pleading causes. Unfair! Latin eloquence, as exemplified by Cicero, could give Demosthenes himself points. Virgil never mentions Cicero—even when Cataline the Criminal, whose revolt Cicero crushed, is prophetically portrayed on the shield of Aeneas; but caricatures him as the abominable "Drances" in the Eleventh Book. Cicero, it must be remembered, who upheld constitutional Republican government, had fallen a victim to Augustus' rough justice. And Virgil himself, on the sole occasion that he pleaded in a Court of Law had, Suetonius says, made a mess of things by speaking "hesitatingly and like an uneducated rustic."

But why should the name of Julius Caesar, Augustus' great-uncle and adoptive father, not be mentioned in the *Aeneid*, either? Was not Julius the most gifted, heroic and magnanimous of all Aeneas' descendants—a supreme orator, too—and the only one who had yet been deified? An oblique reference occurs in Anchises' complaint that one of the Aeneadae is destined to take up arms against his own son-in-law (Pompey), and imbrue the soil with Roman blood. Here Virgil has pandered to Augustus' envy of Julius' wider fame; and makes a pretence of forgetting that Augustus fought a civil war against his brother-in-law Mark Antony. Augustus is oddly hailed as "The Prince of Peace." True, he established peace—by hunting down the last of his Republican opponents. But the divine mystique which Virgil helped to perpetuate for him and his heirs destroyed all safeguards against absolute tyranny; thus fomenting rebellions and further civil wars in subsequent reigns.

Virgil committed a single political blunder. His former patron Gallus, sent by Augustus to Egypt after the Battle of Actium, had obliged four of Antony's legions to surrender, and then defeated Antony so soundly at Paraetonium that he did away with himself. (What became of

Lycoris is not known.) Virgil thought it appropriate to eulogize Gallus in the *Fourth Georgic*. Augustus, however, grew suspicious of his Procurator. Suppose he seized Egypt and starved Rome by holding back the grain-ships? Gallus' enemies, aware of the situation, brought charges of disloyalty against him, and he knew that he was lost. On hearing of his suicide, Virgil cut out the eulogy. Now, as Professor George Duckworth of Princeton has demonstrated beyond all possible doubt, in his recent pamphlet *Mathematical Symmetry in Virgil's Aeneid*, Virgil never consulted the Muse; he only borrowed Apollo's slide-rule. The *Aeneid* is, indeed, craftily built according to a Greek architectural theory known as the Golden Section, or the Divine Proportion, or the Golden Mean Ratio. Virgil, the Apollonian, whose interest in mathematics Suetonius mentions had, Professor Duckworth shows, divided his books into three parts each, relating these parts by the Golden Mean Ratio; and these parts into lesser units, also in the same Divine proportion; and these again into speeches or incidents also in the same proportion, by a deliberate counting of lines and even of half-lines. . . . Thus, to keep the scheme correct and in order, Virgil needed to replace his discarded eulogy of Gallus with a piece of equal length. He used what reads like a discarded poem of pre-*Eclogue* vintage: the intrusive legend of Aristaeus, which has always puzzled the Virgilistae.

It has been noted that, once taken up by Maecenas, Virgil never again mentions Pollio, though he lived to a venerable age. This may be due either to ingratitude or to caution; Gallus and Pollio had been close friends. The *Fourth Eclogue*, which Virgil had addressed to Pollio when he was about to enter on his Consulship, makes a curious story. Virgil here announces that he will "now use a somewhat loftier strain." Observe the "somewhat"; and, indeed, the eclogue is couched in a familiar, bantering style. Pollio has, at last, deserted beautiful boys and sired a son on his lawful wife. Virgil hunts around for a suitable source of felicitation, and finds just the thing in the *Sibylline Oracles*. Everyone who has read early Roman history will recall that the Sibyl of Cumae (seventh century B.C.), to whose thirteenth-century predecessor Aeneas had paid a visit, bullied the Roman King Tarquinius Priscus into buying her stock of manuscript prophecies; which he thereupon placed in the Roman archives, to be consulted whenever danger threatened the State. Unfortunately, these "Sibylline Leaves" got burned during the Sulla-Marius troubles and, seven years before Virgil's birth, commissioners were appointed to secure another set. The burned manuscripts were not, in fact, the Cumaean Sibyl's own work, but borrowed by her from a more ancient prophetess, the Sibyl of Erythrae in Ionia. During their travels through Ionia, Syria and Egypt, the commissioners came across a great many Greek "Sibylline" oracles, which they brought back, sorted and edited. That Virgil had access to this official selection cannot be proved, since Stilicho deliberately destroyed it in the fourth century A.D. But he certainly had access to a mixed bag of others, still extant, drawn from many different countries and historical periods. It happened to be a Graeco-Jewish piece that Virgil chose: one adapting Isaiah's Messianic prophecies to some Egyptian philosophic theory of a new Golden Age which succeeds each new Aeon.

The year of Pollio's consulship was a happy one: Augustus temporarily reconciled with his rival Mark Antony by the mediation of Pollio himself; and Virgil, among others, mistaking this armed truce for an end to civil war. Thus the Sibylline prophecy of a laughing child being born, of the wolf and the lamb lying down together, of the child leading bear and lion on a halter and playing unharmed with the dragon and snake—all under the benignant eye of the Universal Father—delighted Virgil. He borrowed from it piecemeal, and added for good measure excerpts from other prophecies in the same collection. Perhaps, it has been suggested, he was gently burlesquing Pollio's Orientalism.

Two hundred years later, certain Church Fathers read into the *Fourth Eclogue* an original prophecy of the Advent. Augustine and Lactantius made a pre-Christian prophet of Virgil, placing him *in limbo Patrum;* and a legend arose that St. Paul wept on his grave, grieved by the thought that this noble poet had been denied a chance to accept the Cross. As loyal Roman citizens, they would not remove Virgil from his place in the national curriculum; besides, his teachings were, at a pinch, reconcilable with Christianity. Had he not used the myth of a beneficent Father creating the Universe, in preference to Lucretius' Epicurean theory that it came about by a fortuitous combination of atoms? In the *Aeneid*, too, sensual feelings were so little stirred that Aeneas (solemnly obeying the divine voice, rather than his own desires and appetites, in his ditching of Dido) could become a prototype of all heroic saints and missionaries. They also gathered Seneca into the fold—a millionaire philosopher, the Anti-Christ Nero's tutor, and privy to the poisoning of his own patron Claudius—because Seneca had occasionally lifted moral precepts from the New Testament. They even forged a correspondence between him and St. Paul which passed as authentic for a thousand years or more!

Some Churchmen still enlarge on Virgil's having made

the *Fourth Eclogue* "a blue-print of the *Aeneid*, which foreshadows the Christian ideal." But if Christians need to bolster faith in the Gospels by treating the works of Virgil and Seneca as pre-Canonical Scripture, they deserve to have the *hendiadys* quoted at them from Book Two of the *Aeneid*:

Non tali auxilio, nec defensoribus istis . . .

(Not with help such as *that*, not with *those* defenders!)

A strange phenomenon is the counter Virgil invented by a German mediaeval Romance writer: Virgil of Toledo, the great magician who, among other marvels, made himself a talking head. He came into being partly because of Publius Virgilius Maro's ill-deserved fame as a herald of Christ; and partly because the habit of turning the pages of Homer at random and putting one's finger on a line that could be construed as a prophecy, had been successfully applied to Virgil when he displaced Homer in the schools. This counter-Virgil was a *vates*, a dedicated poet, armed with all the magical power appropriate to his calling. On one occasion, imprisoned in a dungeon, he took charcoal and with it drew a galley on the wall, persuading his fellow-captives that this vessel had come to rescue them. They stepped aboard, rowed away, and Virgil, taking the tiller, steered them, fourth-dimensionally, to safety on a mountain top; which is a pretty fair metaphor of what Muse-poems can do for their readers.

Many romantically inclined Classicists, somehow convincing themselves that Virgil was born at Toledo, not at Andes, are tempted to discover *frissons* in the *Aeneid* where none was intended. . . . I am reminded of Professor Loomis' essay on how the ruins of a wholly utilitarian

Roman fort at Segontium near Caernavon, built by
Agricola, became etherialized in mediaeval Welsh legend
as Caer Segeint, then as Caer Seint, and finally as Sinadon
—a golden-roofed hall vaulted with precious stones, where
noble youths sat at chess, and Queen Helen occupied her
throne of pure gold. But it is even worse to be seduced by
such deliberately contrived rhetorical horripilations as:

In summas arces Tritonia—respice—Pallas
Insedit nimbo effulgens et Gorgone saeva.

The Personal Muse

OXFORD CHAIR OF POETRY LECTURE III

Do you complain that I have defined the dedicated poet too narrowly? Do you insist that Virgil, for example, was dedicated to his art of political verse-making, with the surreptitious aid of Pythagoras' Golden Section? And that St. Gregory Nazianzenus was equally dedicated?—the St. Gregory in honour of whose pious lucubrations the Church authorities sought out and burned great stacks of pagan poetry, including Sappho's, as no longer convenient Christian reading? Very well: you are on firm ground. All verse compositions may be loosely called "poems"—the dictionary permits this enlarged sense of the word. One should not forget even the dedicated craftsmen who write pantomime librettos or the mottoes for Christmas crackers.

In my first lecture I distinguished between verse rhetoric, the product of cold reason, and true poetry, the result of an emotional trance. For some three thousand years, the inspiration that accompanies poetic trances has been ascribed to a character called the Muse; and although the meaning of "Muse" has long been blurred by dishonest or facetious usage, what other word can replace it? The original Muse, or Mountain-goddess, whom the pre-

Classical Greeks worshipped on Olympus, Helicon, Parnassus and elsewhere did not, of course, appear by candlelight in a poet's attic and guide his pen; the Muse-trance was a collective one induced at set lunar festivals. The Goddess rode her devotees very much as the voodoo gods of Haiti now ride theirs: causing them to chant and dance ecstatically; though first, no doubt, the tribal poet felt called upon to invoke the Goddess ceremoniously, and provide a ballad refrain—which is still a tribal's poet's task in the South Cameroons and other remote parts of West Africa. In Greece by the eighth century B.C., invocation of the Muse had become a formality—a claim that Sons of Homer could entrance listeners with the harp in a palace courtyard as effectively as when stamp of foot and clap of hand beat out the Goddess' dance rhythms on the slopes of a mountain.

One thing is certain: though countless dull poets in the service of politics, learning, or the Church, have since used this invocation to enlarge their literary fame, true possession by the Muse (a phenomenon which can be neither provoked nor foreseen) does occur sporadically to this day among dedicated poets.

That a Goddess so long banished to wet woods and bramble-bound ruins continues to exert a divine spell is ridiculed not only by churchmen but by scientists who find no room in their macrocosm even for Jehovah. Nevertheless, most anthropologists give primitive gods *de facto* recognition as the alleged sponsors of abnormal psychical phenomena, and welcome the public honour given to modern European poets (unendowed private citizens not even necessarily equipped with university degrees or diplomas) as a tacit acknowledgment of their control by a supernatural power. The Muse cannot, of

course, be ecclesiasticized. Concerted attempts to rebuild
her shrines would be inept, now that she manifests herself not collectively to a group of devotees, but to the
individual poet in privacy. Although his poems may be
on public sale, the readers are individuals and study them
apart, also.in privacy.

It is difficult to discuss the Muse concept in historic
terms. Let me begin by saying that a deity must remain
an idle abstraction, unless he or she has (to employ West
African terms) a *sunsum* as well as a *kra—kra* meaning
supernatural power, *sunsum* meaning an agreed person-
ality. A *sunsum* becomes so notable that the devotee
"ridden" by, say, the goddess Ntoa or the god Odoman-
koma, uses certain traditional gestures, tones and manner-
isms at once recognized as the deity's own. Consider the
Hebrew prophets—"prophet" means "one who speaks on
behalf of God," not necessarily "one who forecasts the
future." Though we cannot be sure whether, when acting
as mouthpieces of the Palestinian Bull-god El, they adopted
his *sunsum*, or merely claimed his *kra*, yet the Bible de-
clares that genuine divine possession could be distinguished
from false. We know that Zedekiah the son of Chenaanah
impersonated El by providing himself with horns of iron,
and that he cried: "Thus shalt thou push the Assyrians!";
but we are told that the god was clearly not riding him
at the time.

When a pseudo-poet claims to be inspired by his Muse,
the case is much the same. True poetic trances excite
memorable images, strong personal rhythms, and a peculiar syntax which, together, transcend in emotional
force the most considered rhetoric; false trances imitate
these elements, but deceive no reader of sensibility. I

wrote on the subject of pseudo-poets some years ago in a poem titled *Any Honest Housewife:*

Any honest housewife could sort them out,
Having a nose for fish, an eye for apples.
Is it any mystery who are the sound
And who the rotten? Never, by her lights.

Any honest housewife who by ill-fortune
Ever engaged a slut to scrub for her
Could instantly distinguish from the workers
The lazy, the liars, and the petty thieves.

Does this denote a sixth peculiar sense
Gifted to housewives for their vestal needs?
Or is it failure of the usual five
In all unthrifty writers on this head?

And any honest dedicated poet, with a nose and an eye, will take up a new volume of verse, riffle the pages through, and decide after two minutes, by a pricking of his finger-tips, whether or not the Muse has been in attendance. His tasks are to recognize her *kra* and her *sunsum;* never to write (if he can help it) except under her influence; and never to praise poems otherwise written. Attempts to supplant the Muse by worshipping Apollo have always failed—Apollo being a patron of the intellect, not of intuitive truth: of metre, not of rhythm; of novelty, not of timelessness.

Fifteen years ago, when I wrote *The White Goddess,* I tried to put the Muse's *sunsum* and *kra* into clearer focus by examining her ancient rites, and reminiscences of them found in European folklore and myth. I came to the conclusion that the main theme of her worship still rules the dedicated poet. Some of you have read the book,

most of you have not; so those who have must please
excuse my quoting three short paragraphs from it.

The Theme, briefly, recounts the birth, life, death and
resurrection of the Demigod of the Waxing Year; the
central chapters concern his losing fight against the Demigod of the Waning Year, his rival for love of the all-
powerful and inscrutable Threefold Goddess, their
mother, bride and layer-out. The poet identifies himself
with the Demigod of the Waxing Year; the rival is his
twin, his second self, his weird. All true poetry—true by
A. E. Housman's practical razor test: "Does it make the
hairs of one's chin bristle if one repeats it silently while
shaving?"—celebrates some incident or other of this ancient story; and the three main characters are so much a
part of our racial legacy that they also assert themselves
in dreams and paranoiac visions.

The rival sometimes appears as the tall, lean, dark-faced
spectre, or Prince of the Air, who tries to drag a dreamer
out through the window, so that he looks back at this
body lying rigid in bed; but he takes countless other
malevolent or diabolic or serpent-like forms. The Goddess is a lovely, slender woman who will suddenly trans-
form herself into sow, bitch, mare, vixen, she-ass, weasel,
serpent, owl, she-wolf, tigress, mermaid or loathsome hag.
Her names and titles are multifold. In ghost stories she
often figures as "The White Lady," and in ancient religions
as the "White Goddess." I can think of no true poet from
Homer onwards who has not recorded his personal experience of her. The test of a poet's vision, one might say,
is the accuracy of his portrayal of the White Goddess, and
of the secret island over which she rules. The hairs stand
on end, the eyes water, the throat constricts, the skin
crawls, and a shiver runs down the spine when one writes

or reads a true poem: because this is necessarily an invocation of the White Goddess, or Muse, the Mother of All Living, the ancient power of love and terror—the female spider or the queen-bee whose courtship means murder. Housman offered an alternative test of true poetry: whether it matches a phrase of Keats's, "everything that reminds me of her goes through me like a spear." This has equal pertinence to the Theme: Keats was writing under the shadow of death about his personal Muse, Fanny Brawne; and "the spear that roars for blood" is the traditional weapon of the dark executioner and supplanter.

Sometimes the hairs will bristle at an apparently unpeopled and eventless scene, if the elements bespeak the Goddess' hidden presence clearly enough: for example, when owls hoot, the moon rides like a ship through scudding cloud, trees sway slowly together above a rushing waterfall, and a distant barking of dogs is heard; or when a peal of bells in frosty weather suddenly announces the birth of a New Year. . . . Despite the deep, sensory satisfaction that some readers derive from Classical poetry, it never makes the hair rise or the heart leap, except perhaps where the verseman has failed to maintain decorous composure; and this marks the difference between the attitudes to the White Goddess of Apollonian poets and dedicated poets.

The Ugarit Epic, discovered at Ras Shamra in 1926, supplies one ancient text of the Theme. Two demi-gods, Aleyan and Mot, fall in love with Anatha—*alias* Neith, a pre-dynastic Libyan goddess. Aleyan is the Bright Twin; Mot is the Dark Twin. Although the Ras Shamra tablets are fragmentary at a crucial point, we gather from analogous myths that Anatha encouraged Mot to murder his

Bright Twin Aleyan, and then went off with him. As a
result, all grass and herbs languished and a universal lam-
entation arose. Anatha then thought again, and avenged
Aleyan's death by the destruction of Mot, whose body
she ground in a mill, leaving the remains to carrion birds.
Finally she harrowed Hell, rescued Aleyan, and set him
on his throne again. The Goddess' betrayal of the Bright
Twin is a constant element in Hebrew, Greek and Celtic
myth. An early non-Biblical Hebrew tradition even makes
Cain murder Abel for the favours of another Eve—*alias*
Hepta, or Hipatu, a Hittite goddess identified with Anatha.

The Theme originally concerned a seasonal war between the Spirit of Growth and the Demon of Drought.
It seems that at the barley harvest, when the blazing
Palestinian sun dried up all grass and herbs, Anatha, incarnate in a priestess-queen, annually ordered the cruci-
fixion of her sacred consort as a means of placating the
Demon of Drought; then took the executioner into her
bed until the autumn rains should come—after which she
destroyed him, chose another sacred king: in theory, the
crucified man risen from the dead. This ritual practice
ceased when the patriarchal cattle people swept down
from the north-east, over-running the queendoms; and a
Bull-king, or Father-god, gradually assumed the Goddess'
powers. But the Theme survived in Hebrew myth and
ritual. It even appears, transmogrified, in the Christian
doctrine of the sacred king, betrayed by his own familiar
friend, who died crucified at the harvest festival for love
not of the Goddess but of the Father-god.

Orthodox Christianity marks a parting of ways between
poets who serve the Muse, and non-poets who inherit
from the patriarchal Hebrew prophets a mistrust of

woman as the temptress: prime cause of man's fall from divine grace. By asserting an irrepressible confidence in woman, as being closer to the divine than man, the poet imaginatively casts himself for the rôle of the sacred king destined to die at his queen's command. And the early mediaeval Church, recognizing a widespread homesickness for the Goddess, shrewdly gave this emotion vent by the sanction of Mariolatry: though extolling Mary as a virgin without blemish, and denying her membership in the Divine Trinity. Catholic poets have accepted this compromise; but the poet for whom the Muse, so far from being a virgin, presides over physical passion, will continue to pledge her his eternal faith, arbitrary and merciless though she may seem—an attitude which appears evil to Christians, and morbid to philosophers. His is a wholehearted protest against the patriarchal system: in so far as it values the intellect at the expense of instinct; and force at the expense of persuasion; and written laws at the expense of custom.

A dedicated poet sees history as a dangerous deviation from the true course of human life—an attempt to deny women their age-old moral ascendancy. A poet's absolute love, his readiness to trust in woman's wisdom, whatever may ensue, represents a nostalgia for human truth. He does not, however, love indiscriminately, but only *the* woman, the royal woman, an incarnation of the Goddess, gifted with her *kra*, who (he assures himself) is waiting somewhere to restore the lost mysteries of mankind. From this obsessive love of an unknown Muse proceed poems of trance, in which the ancient mythical elements assemble thickly. The Muse, I have said, is "the perpetual other woman," never the poet's wife; meaning that the poet-

Muse relationship either precedes the patriarchal system, or looks forward to an epoch which must succeed it. Patriarchal marriage would put the Muse under his moral sway, a circumstance impossible for her to accept.

The only Christian country where a tradition of equal love between the sexes survived in the Dark Ages was Ireland. The Irish Church, having been planted by Eastern missionaries, escaped Papal interference. Kings chose bishops from among their dependents, assigning them lands for individual tenure, not in the form of Church property; and the Ollamhs, or master-poets, the chief Councillors of State, still worshipped the Triple-goddess Bridget (of Poetry, Medicine and Smithcraft) in thin Christian disguise. Noble Irish women were known to have minds of their own, and encouraged to use them, as can be seen from such dramatic tales as Cuchulain's wooing of Emer, Midir's wooing of Étain, Deirdre's mourning for Naoise, the loves of Liadan and Curithir, of Créide and Cáel. The intensity of Irish love passion is shown in this ninth-century poem from *Midir's Wooing of Étain*:

> Torment I have endured a twelvemonth,
> With grief well hidden behind my eyes,
> With strength enlarged beyond belief
> To the four quarters of this earth,
> To the highest crown of heaven.
>
> Love is a breaking of the neck-bone
> In battle with a spectre,
> Love is a drowning in flood water,
> Love is a race against the nightly stars,
> Or hero-feats below the salt sea.
> I wooed the echo in wooing her,
> To whom, body and soul, I bound myself.

Nevertheless, the Irish poet's beloved was always presented as a woman, not a goddess—unless in plainly mythical tales, like *Oisin and Niamh of the Golden Hair* and *Grainne and Diarmat*. This unorthodox Irish view of woman as something more than a mere sexual or domestic convenience, as having thoughts and sensibilities worthy of man's close regard, came to England at third hand after the Norman Conquest: when Welsh minstrel traditions of Irish origin were woven by Breton bards into the Norman-French Arthurian romances—*Tristan and Iseult*, for example, being a version of *Grainne and Diarmat;* and *Gawain and the Green Knight* of *Cuchulain and Curoi.*

An equally important source of English love-poetry was Provence, with its extensions to Northern Spain and Italy. Many untruths are current about the troubadors—taken from Catholic propaganda against the Albigensian heresy, to which many of them seem to have been attached. These poets, of whom one hundred and eleven figure in the records, and who included twenty-three ruling princes, among them Richard Coeur de Lion, flourished from the early twelfth century to the late thirteenth, and celebrated a view of human love that cut across ecclesiastical tradition. Such sacred power was claimed for the extra-marital bond which united a troubador to his beloved, that Bernart of Ventadour—a former scullion but a leading troubador—suffered only banishment when his amours with the Viscountess of Montluçon came to light. And when the jealous Count of Castel-Roussillon murdered Guillem de Capestang, and caused Seremonda, his countess, to commit suicide by serving up Guillem's heart for her supper, all Provence rose to avenge the lovers; and pilgrims flocked to the grave in Perpignan Cathedral, where their

bodies had been laid together. The adulterous loves of
Guinevere and Lancelot were treated as sacred in the
Morte d'Arthur as late as the fifteenth century; and Lord
Barnard, of the Border ballad, after killing his wife and
Little Musgrave when he found them making love to-
gether, laments that he has done away with the finest
couple of all England. Women poets appeared among the
troubadors, as they appeared in early mediaeval Ireland;
one of them, Eleanor of Guienne, became Henry II's
Queen.

The usual etymology of *troubador* is the Provençal
word *trobar*, "to find or invent"; an alternative suggestion
is the Latin *turbare*, "to stir up"; but since the editors of
the *Oxford English Dictionary* are unwilling, on linguistic grounds, to accept either of these, I incline to the
view that *troubador* represents the Arabic *ta rabub*, "lute
player." Historians often casually mention the troubadors' debt to Arabic poets; but the Arabs were not lovers
in this sacred sense. The troubadors' real debt was to
Sufism—a way of thought refined by the Persians and
eventually adapted to Islam, though in essence heretical.
Moorish invasions of Spain and Southern France had
brought along a heterogenous mass of Islamic visitors
from distant Oriental lands—traces of whose cults are to
be found not only in *flamenco* dancing (of Yemenite, not
gipsy origin), but in the mediaeval witch records of Spain,
France and Britain. By the twelfth century, Morisco
lutanists clad in motley and with bells on their ankles, had
gone all through Provence singing love-ditties based on
the Persian; from these the troubadors, it seems, learned
their code of behaviour.

The Sufis seek to eliminate by a long course of mental

discipline whatever desires and beliefs are foreign to divine love. A Sufi feels superior to normal restraints and, being spiritually and physically at one with the woman who has accepted his devotion, claims a certitude that allows him to face every danger and bring seeming impossibilities to pass. Sufic thought, though its spiritual disciplines appear to have been scamped in Provence, contributed to the Albigensian heresy, against which the Catholic Church directed all the armies she could muster, in the bloodiest of Holy Wars. Church historians libel the troubadors. Thus Guillem of Poitiers, Duke of Aquitaine, is said to have roved the country seducing noblewomen with his songs; and William of Malmesbury even accuses him of having intended to found a religious house for Venus worship. Ritual sodomy is also charged against them; though nothing more plainly heterosexual than their love could be conceived. A familiar stanza of Omar Khayyam's Persian *Rubaiyat* offers a clue to this error. Omar writes:

A book of verses under the bough.
A loaf of bread, a flask of wine, and Thou
Beside me singing in the wilderness—
And wilderness were Paradise enow.

English readers, told that the "Thou" is masculine, are apt to imagine an old sensualist swigging wine in the shade, while a pretty choirboy provides musical accompaniment. But "bread" was the Persian emblem of wisdom, and "wine" of ecstasy; and "Thou" was the poet's beloved woman. For Sufic convention gave her a masculine gender, to show that the bond between a poet and his love should transcend, even if it includes, ordinary sexual commerce.

The troubadors' heretical convictions were decently ecclesiasticized when Petrarch, a clerk in Holy Orders, professed a chaste love for Laura de Noyes, Hugo de Sade's wife—after which a living Muse could encourage her poet with a distant smile, as it might be the image of a Virgin Martyr miraculously made flesh, yet not allow him so much as a hand-clasp of intimate understanding. And though Petrarch might be accused of harbouring illegitimate desires for Laura's person, his successor Dante guarded himself against a similar charge by a more prudent choice of Muse. He had felt a sudden pang of divine love for Beatrice when both of them were only nine years old; but so far as anyone knows, she never reciprocated his feelings or considered herself in the least degree affected by them. Beatrice bore her husband twelve children, and Dante had some of his own—yet even her death could not remove his obsession. Thus, despite his vehement praise, in the *Inferno*, of the troubador Arnaut Daniel, the new theory of Courtly Love remained artificial and unreal: an "Inamorato's Manual: every man his own Muse."

Sir Thomas Wyatt was the first Englishman to imitate Italian, French and Spanish verse models of Courtly Love. His titles tell the story:

The Lover for Shamefastness Hideth His Desire Within His Faithful Heart . . .

The Lover Waxeth Wiser, and Will Not Die for Affection . . .

The Abused Lover Seeth His Folly and Intendeth to Trust no More . . .

The Lover Describeth His Being Stricken With Sight of His Love . . .

The Wavering Lover Willeth, and Dreadeth, to Move His Desire . . .

How the Lover Perisheth in His Delight as the Fly in the Fire . . .

The Lover Despairing to Attain Unto His Lady's Grace, Relinquisheth the Pursuit . . .

The Deserted Lover Consoleth Himself with Remembrance that All Women Are by Nature Fickle . . .

The Deserted Lover Wisheth that His Rival Might Experience the Same Fortune He Himself Had Tasted . . .

The Neglected Lover Calleth on His Stony Hearted Mistress to Hear Him Complain Ere that He Die . . .

The Lover Having Broken His Bondage, Voweth Never More to Be Enthralled . . .

The Abused Lover Admonishes the Unwary to Beware of Love . . .

Deserted by His Mistress, He Renounceth All Joy for Ever . . .

These were graceful exercises describing different clinical stages in the fever of love, and despite a pretence of Petrarchian chastity, proved ingenious sexual lures. The Muse being both anonymous and impersonal, they could all be addressed to any woman willing to take a hand in the love game. By thus serenading susceptible Court ladies, Wyatt won numerous intimate favours; and seems neither to have loved openly in the chivalrous manner of the troubadors, flaunting his beloved's kerchief on his casque, nor to have dedicated himself to the divine Muse. Few of these poems stand out as honestly his own. An exception is *The Recovered Lover Exulteth in His Freedom*, which begins:

I am as I am, and so will I be,
But how that I am, none knoweth trewely—
Be it evil, be it well, be I loved, be I free,
I am as I am, and so will I be.

But how that is, I leave to you—
Judge as ye list, false or true,
Ye know no more than afore ye knew
Yet I am as I am, whatever ensue.

None "knoweth trewely," in fact, what his game is—not
even the many women to whom he has dedicated himself
heart and soul. *The Faithful Lover Wisheth All Evil May
Befall Him if He Forsake His Lady* reads typically:

The knot which first my heart did strain,
When that your servant I becam,
Doth bind me still for to remain,
Always your own as now I am;
And if you find that now I feign,
With just judgemént myself I damn,
To have disdain.

If other thought in me do grow
But still to love you steadfastly;
If that the proof do not well show
That I am yours assuredly;
Let every wealth turn me to woe,
And you to be continually
My chiefest foe . . .

If in my love there be one spot
Of false deceit or doubleness;
Or if I mind to slip the knot
By want of faith or steadfastness;
Let all my service be forgot,
And when I would have chief redress,
Esteem me not . . .

And for the end of this my song,
Unto your hands I do submit
My deadly grief, and pains so strong
Which in my heart be firmly shut,
And when ye list, redress my wrong:
Since well ye know this painful fit
Hath last too long.

Too glib a statement to carry conviction, and never so intended! And at the end, when Wyatt had outgrown his amorous escapades, he fell back on self-pity. The one woman is now revealed as "they": *The Lover Showeth How He Is Forsaken of Such as He Sometime Enjoyed.*

They flee from me that sometime did me seek,
    With naked foot stalking within my chamber:
Once have I seen them gentle, tame, and meek,
    That now are wild, and do not once remember
    That sometime they have put themselves in danger
To take bread at my hand; and now they range
Busily seeking in continual change.

Thanked be Fortúne, it hath been otherwise,
    Twenty times better; but once inespecial,
In thin array, after a pleasant guise,
    When her loose gown did from her shoulders fall,
    And she me caught in her arms long and small,
And therewithal so sweetly did me kiss,
And softly said: "Dear heart, how like you this?"

It was no dream; for I lay broad awaking:
    But all is turned, thorough my gentleness,
Into a strangë fashion of forsaking;
    And I have leave to go of her goodnéss,
    And she also to use new-fangleness:
But since that I so kindly am servèd:
I would fain know what she had déservèd?

John Donne likewise used love-poems as a means of seduction. He persuaded himself, at times, of his love's absoluteness; yet, when the flame had died down, declared that the spiritual identity of lovers was an illusion. His poems yield no portraits of individual women; their bright eyes always reflect his own passionate image. One of his loves, we read, sent him amusing letters, but he does not quote a line from them; and if he kept their identities secret, roundly cursing any man who guessed the secret, it was himself whom he feared to compromise.

The series begins boldly with *The Good Morrow:*

I wonder by my troth, what thou and I
Did, till we loved? Were we not weaned till then,
But sucked on country pleasures childishly?
Or snorted we in the seven sleepers' den?
T'was so; but this, all pleasures fancies be.
If ever any beauty, I did see,
Which I desired, and got, t'was but a dream of thee.

And now good morrow to our waking souls,
Which watch not one another out of fear;
For love, all love of other sights controls,
And makes one little room an everywhere.
Let sea-discovers to new worlds have gone,
Let Maps to other, worlds on worlds have showne,
Let us possess one world, each hath one, and is one.

My face is thine eye, thine in mine appears,
And true plain hearts do in the faces rest,
Where can we find two better hemispheres
Without sharp North, without declining West?
Whatever dies was not mixed equally;
If our two loves be one, or thou and I
Love so alike that none do slacken, none can die.

But soon doubt creeps in; one woman is no better than another, and all are faithless. He writes in *The Indifferent:*

I can love both fair and brown,
Her whom abundance melts, and her whom want betrays,
Her who loves loneness best, and her who masks and
    plays,
Her whom the country formed, and whom the town,
Her who believes, and her who tries,
Her who still weeps with spongy eyes,
And her who is dry cork and never cries;
I can love her, and her, and you and you,
I can love any, so she be not true . . .

The first stanza of *Air and Angels* does not deny his
doubt. The Muse, he explains, is his own imaginative creation, not a power recognized by him:

Twice or thrice had I loved thee,
Before I knew thy face or name;
So in a voice, so in a shapeless flame,
Angels affect us oft, and worshipped be;
Still when to where thou wert I came,
Some lovely glorious nothing I did see.
    But since my soul, whose child Love is,
Takes limbs of flesh, and else could nothing do,
    More subtil than the parent is
Love must not be, but take a body too.
    And therefore what thou wert, and who,
        I bid Love ask, and now
That it assume thy body I allow
And fix itself in thy lip, eye, and brow . . .

He allows himself an occasional glimpse of what absolute
love can mean in these stanzas from *A Valediction:*

Dull sublunary lovers' love
    (Whose soul is sense) cannot admit
Absence, because it doth remove
    Those things which elemented it.

But we by a love so much refined
  That our selves know not what it is,
Inter-assuréd of the mind,
  Care less, eyes, lips, and hands to miss.

Our two souls therefore, which are one,
  Though I must go, endure not yet
A breach, but an expansión,
  Like gold to airy thinness beat . . .

Absence, indeed, seems more rewarding to him than presence, when presence is the erotic abandon which he celebrates in his *Nineteenth Elegy* but depreciates in his
Farewell to Love:

                    . . . the thing which lovers so
Blindly admire, and with such worship woo;
  Being had, enjoying it decays:
    And thence
What before pleased them all, takes but one sense,
  And that so lamely as it leaves behind
A kind of sorrowing dullness to the mind.

He confesses in *Love's Alchemy:*

Some that have deeper digged love's mine than I,
Say where this centrique happiness doth lie:
  I have loved, and got, and told,
But should I love, get, tell, till I were old,
I should not find the hidden mystery;
  Oh, 'tis imposture all . . .

Hope not for mind in women; at their best
Sweetness and wit, they are but *Mummy*, possessed.

And *The Token* shows that he does not expect the woman
addressed to trust him:

... I beg no ribband wrought with thine own hands,
  To knit our loves in the fantastic strain
Of new-touched youth; nor ring to shew the strands
  Of our affection, that, as that's round and plain,
So should our loves meet in simplicity.
  No, nor the corals which thy wrist enfold,
Laced up together in congruity
  To show your thoughts should rest in the same hold;
No, nor thy picture, though most gracious,
  And most desired, because best like the best;
Nor witty lines, which are most copious,
  Within the writings which thou hast addressed.

Send me nor this, nor that, to increase my store,
But swear thou thinkst I love thee, and no more.

She had been warned in his *Elegy:*

I love her well and would, if need were, die
To do her service. But follows it that I
Must serve her only, when I may have choice
Of other beauties, and in change rejoice?

"I would die to do her service" is rhetorical; Donne remained uncommitted. Later, he married well; proved a faithful husband; took Holy Orders; and, after his wife's death, gave his heart to the Father-god and duly repented his sins. He writes in *A Hymn to God the Father:*

Wilt Thou forgive that sin by which I have won
  Others to sin and made my sin their door?
Wilt Thou forgive that sin which I did shun
  A year or two: but wallowed in, a score?
    When Thou hast done, Thou hast not done,
            For I have more.

I have a sin of fear, that when I have spun
  My last thread, I shall perish on the shore;
Swear by Thyself, that at my death Thy Son

Shall shine as he shines now and heretofore;
And, having done that, Thou hast done,
I fear no more.

Must I take you through all the corpus to prove that
the Tudor poet had little thought for the women he
celebrated save as beautiful, complaisant bedfellows—no
respect for their mind, pride or sensibility; and that if
they would not succumb to his blandishments, he felt
aggrieved? An anonymous poem in *Tottel's Miscellany* is
put into a Court lady's mouth:

Girt is my guiltless gown, as I sit here and sew,
I see that things are not in deed as to the outward
show . . .

She then speaks of a love-song:

The author whereof came, wrapped in a crafty cloak
In will to force a flaming fire where he could raise no
smoke.
If power and will had met, as it appeareth plain,
Nor truth nor right had ta'en a place—their virtues had
been vain.

But even poets who love humanly with all their heart's
affection, and those who idealize women as distant saints,
alike avoid the third and most poetic way of love: namely
the recognition of the Muse-goddess as incarnate in some
particular woman, who must be loved and trusted whatever
happens. Though a sudden sense of the Goddess' creative
power may overcome a poet when he first falls in love, and
be enhanced by his rediscovery of her ancient titles and
emblems, only a personal Muse can open the arcana of
poetry to him.

Royal women are rare—wild, ruthless, awe-inspiring,

their progress like a forest fire—the greener the wood, the fiercer the flames. For "royal" let me substitute "real": they are the same word originally. Was Donne incapable of the absolute love demanded by such a Muse because male pride would not let him yield to it? Or did he never meet a woman real enough to subdue his pride? In my view he knew what this love meant, but deliberately rejected it; so that the Muse who should have claimed him as her poet, and saved his soul, went frowning away. Donne's punishment appears in an abject address to *The Father*:

Father of Heaven, and Him by whom
It and us, for it, and all else, for us
   Thou mad'st, and govern'st ever, come
And re-create me, now grown ruinous:
   My heart is by dejection, clay,
   And by self-murder, red.
From this red earth, O Father, purge away
All vicious tinctures, that new fashionèd
I may rise up from death, before I'm dead.

Strangely enough, the woman who came nearest to a true personal Muse in Tudor times was Queen Elizabeth herself, as celebrated by Sir Walter Raleigh. Though he has been accused of flattery, self-seeking and other ignoble traits in his relations with Elizabeth (who was almost twenty years older than he) and though his earlier poems of prosperity in love have disappeared, leaving only complaints of her subsequent unkindness, it is difficult after reading *The Eleventh and Last Book of the Ocean to Cynthia* to challenge the reality of the power she exercised over his heart. And the most compelling of all Muse poems in English, *The Holy Land of Walsingham*, is Raleigh's.

A tremendous effort of will freed early historic man from subservience to a matriarchate. Breaking the female monopoly of arts, sciences, and religious ritual, he consolidated his gains by a development of intellect, until he had made women his chattels. By a tremendous effort of intellect he achieved the power of personal choice. Modern men cannot be expected to renounce this hardly won power, and sell themselves back into collective slavery. But they can perhaps be persuaded that the a-moral exercise of intellect has created institutions hostile to human happiness—total wars, uncontrolled money, denatured food, soul-destroying machines, academicism, commercialized entertainment—which is no great advance on prehistoric savagery.

As I see it, a poet has only one choice: to refrain from exploiting a bovine will-power—from forcing events to adopt intellectually conceived, and therefore unnatural, and therefore disastrous, patterns; and, instead, learn from his Muse how to cultivate an intuitive certitude about the fortunate course of whatever he feels impelled to do. In a recent poem of mine, a lover addresses the Goddess:

Your sceptre rules me, Aphrodite,
The knot-of-wisdom in your grasp . . .

This knot-of-wisdom, or the true lover's knot, is made of two cords so intertwined that the harder one tugs, the more tightly they knit together. West-African queen-mothers carry silver knot-of-wisdom sceptres, meaning "My decisions are irrevocable." Yet their decisions are not mere exercises of female will-power; they represent the natural certitude of rightness given them by the *kra* of their ancestress, the Threefold Moon-goddess Nyame.

Education tends to destroy this intuitive gift in women. Real women are those who resist patriarchal conditioning, and are thus recognized by poets as holding the sceptre tight in their grasp. The Muse, no longer a collective emanation, but incarnate as an inspired, real woman, can teach her poet how to cultivate the same certitude without damaging either his male self-esteem or his male intellect. And it may happen that, before long, a few dedicated poets, by imparting this knowledge to their fellow-men, will change the present disagreeable climate of human thought. Such, at least, is my faith; the only alternative seems to be universal catastrophe.

Many of you will know what I mean by "certitude," though your experience of it is perhaps limited to a small, private, intuitive art in which you shine—you neither know, nor ask, where the magic comes from—but which, if practised with any other object than its own perfection, slowly vanishes. And most of you must occasionally have felt, at some time or other, a peculiar sense of being "on the beam": nothing can go wrong, all your impulses are right. If you throw a stone at a tin can fifty yards away, you cannot fail to score a direct hit—because you have not mathematically computed the distance, the weight of the stone, and other problems of ballistics, but used your sense of divine assurance. I tend to choose my closest friends among those who preserve this faculty in a high degree.

The personal Muse, then, should inspire a poet with her own certitude; in return, he should acknowledge her divine *kra*, though loving her as a woman with a *sunsum* of her own. There is no cabalistic or occult element in such poet-Muse relationships, however difficult they may be to achieve and maintain. At this point I am no longer addressing a general University audience, but talking in an aside to any poets who may be listening. So few are to be found in the elder or middle generations that, doubtless, some younger ones must be growing up whose names are unknown to me. Though Donne's reasons for keeping the name of his beloved concealed do not seem to have been the right ones, the principle was right in so far as the public identification of a woman with a poet's Muse may cause her to reject him as a threat to her private royalty—because people will not readily abandon the notion that whoever actually writes the poems is the more important partner in this difficult relationship, and may persist in regarding her as a mere idol rather than the director.

Too many irresponsible young women, eager for Muse-ship, go in search of poetic recognition. Unless they have the integrity, ruthlessness, and certitude characteristic of a real Muse, they will get entangled with pseudo-poets; and the outcome is always sad, often sordid. Cunning pseudo-poets ruthlessly exploit a pseudo-Muse's innocent ambitions. Real Muses are rare indeed; and not enviable, for the ancient Irish Triad is as true today as ever it was:

> It is death to mock a poet;
> Death to love a poet;
> Death to be a poet.

Here is a message to would-be Muses—*Beware, Madam!*

> Beware, madam, of the witty devil,
> The arch intriguer who walks disguised
> In a poet's cloak, his gay tongue oozing evil.

Would you be a Muse? He will so declare you,
Pledging his blind allegiance,
Yet remain secret and uncommitted.

Poets are men: are single-hearted lovers
Who adore and trust beyond all reason,
Who die honourably at the gates of hell.

The Muse alone is licensed to do murder
And to betray: weeping with honest tears
She thrones each victim in her paradise.

But from this Muse the Devil borrows an art
That ill becomes a man. Beware, madam:
He plots to strip you bare of woman-pride.

He is capable of seducing your twin-sister
On the same pillow, and neither she nor you
Will suspect the act, so close a glamour he sheds.

Alas, being honourably single-hearted,
You adore and trust beyond all reason,
Being no more a Muse than he is a poet.

A poet may likewise be mistaken in his Muse: she may
prove unworthy of continued trust. I have written about
this, too—*In Her Praise:*

This they know well: the Goddess yet abides.
Though each new lovely woman whom she rides,
Straddling her neck a year, or two, or three,
Should sink beneath such weight of majesty
And, groping back to humankind, betray
The headlong power that whitened all her way
With a broad track of trefoil—leaving you
Her chosen lover, ever again thrust through
With daggers, your purse rifled, your rings gone;

Nevertheless they call you to live on,
To parley with the pure, oracular dead,
To hear the wild pack whimpering overhead,
To watch the moon tugging at her cold tides.
Woman is mortal woman. She abides.

I read the story of Anatha, Aleyan and Mot not only as
an ancient seasonal myth, but as a prophecy of this new,
peculiar, not yet fully explored, poet-Muse relationship.
Anatha may well discipline Aleyan for showing signs of
marital possessiveness: may betray him with his cruel,
destructive twin as a means of asserting her personal freedom. But if Aleyan survives the ordeal, after dying cheer-
fully for her sake, she will surely—he tells himself—raise
him up again and destroy his rival. We are no longer, of
course, annually subjected to semi-famine by the droughts
of summer or the frosts of winter. In a city we scarcely
notice the passing of the seasons, and can fly from polar
cold to equatorial heat in a matter of hours, so that the
seasonal myth on which the Theme rests has lost its cursed
absoluteness. But the poet as Sacred King cannot avoid a
love-ordeal which puts his sense of certitude to the
supreme test. And I believe, despite all adverse evidence,
that there was never an epoch in which so many young
men were willing to be ruled by the knot-of-wisdom
sceptre—the royal pledge of absolute if unpredictable love
to those worthy of it.

Poetry does not deny the intellect, or the discipline of
reason: but transcends both. Young poets are often
tempted to despise the formal University curriculum: I
think them mistaken. A curriculum is what one makes of
it. As we say of food in Majorca: "What does not poison,
fattens," and the curriculum is non-poisonous, if in parts

somewhat indigestible. Moreover, Oxford happens to own a peculiar *báraka*, or blessedness—a kindly, non-doctrinaire, generous spirit, unmatched anywhere else in the world. Enjoy it, maintain it!

Poetic Gold

ADDRESS TO THE OXFORD UNIVERSITY
PHILOLOGICAL SOCIETY

My grandfather Charles Graves, afterwards Bishop of Limerick, won the Chancellor's Gold Medal at Trinity College, Dublin, in the eighteen-thirties; so did his two brothers, Robert Graves the physician who became famous for identifying Graves's Disease, and John Graves the Classical historian and lexicographer. These three medals, big as silver dollars and engraved by a Dublin jeweller, hung behind our drawing-room grand piano when I was a child, set in a gilt glass case against a shamrock of faded green velvet. My mother fondly hoped that since her three sons bore the same Christian names, they would one day win three medals of equal importance; yet, each in turn, we disappointed her. We all came up here to St. John's and none of us brought home any University prize whatsoever. "One ought not to consider the intrinsic value of the gold," she moralized, "because it would be wrong to sell or pawn such a medal even if on the point of starvation. Only the achievement counts. Still, gold is the noblest of metals and signifies the honour in which outstanding talents are held."

This piece of family history explains why, in January 1960, I felt my mother's ghost present with me at the

Waldorf-Astoria, New York, where the National Poetry
Society of America were celebrating their Golden Jubilee.
Though an Englishman, I had been judged worthy of the
Prince Alexander Droutzkoy Memorial Award: a gold
medal for Services to Poetry. An alarming experience,
since I have always considered poetry as a private and,
indeed, almost anti-social obsession, and been at pains to
discount its more public manifestations. There I was, in
evening dress, among six hundred fellow-obsessionists as
well-groomed as myself, sitting down to dinner in the
great Sbert Banqueting Hall. The Committee had placed
me with a row of award-winners on a lofty daïs.

The Society's medals and diplomas all carried money
prizes—an aggregate of some six thousand dollars—but,
on studying the list, I noticed that their cash value seldom
corresponded with their billing. In fact, the greater the
honour, as a rule, the less the cash. One certain deduction
was that gold ranked higher than silver, and silver than
bronze, as at trade and agricultural shows.

Robert Frost, the Society's Honorary President, sat near
me, making mischievous *sotto voce* comments. I have
known and loved him since 1914, when we first met ac-
cidentally in a London bookshop; and his carefree mood
gave me courage. Marianne Moore, whom I had not
known before, but always respected for her unchanging
dry wit, was there too; and when the noble Jubilee Birthday Cake came sailing in, flash-bulbs illumined the three
of us bending together over it. Even a much bigger cake
would hardly have gone far among six hundred guests;
still, I was surprised when Miss Moore, who had cut a
ritual slice and blown out most of the fifty candles (Robert Frost pinched out the rest with practised fingers), did
not receive so much as a single crumb or currant. The

Birthday Cake sailed back to the kitchens: to be patched
up, perhaps, for a subsequent Jubilee Celebration of Den-
tists, Wood-Whittlers, or Turkey-Raisers. . . . The surprised look on Miss Moore's face reminded me of Lewis
Carroll's Alice when introduced to the Lobster at the
White Queen's banquet: "Alice—Lobster; Lobster—Alice!
Waiter, remove the Lobster!"

Dr. Clarence B. Decker, the genial President, glanced at
a sheaf of congratulatory cables from all over the world,
and read out President Eisenhower's: to the effect that
poets are vital to American progress, culture and spiritual
endeavour. This being, however, a strictly national occasion, Dr. Decker did not read us a cable from the Secretary of the Russian Union of Writers, which declared
that poets are vital to international culture, peace and
goodwill.

After Dr. Decker had reported on the Society's fifty
years of achievement, Robert Frost spoke in more personal tones about poetry. The awards were then distributed—Miss Moore won a great bronze medal engraved with a Pegasus—and some winners read their prize
poems aloud. My turn came last. Dr. Decker pinned the
Prince Alexander Droutzkoy Memorial Award for Services to Poetry on my lapel, everyone applauded, and I
rose to speak—"for twenty-five minutes or so, if you don't
mind; and please remember the microphone! Our Celebration is being broadcast to five million listeners."

Well, I had won a gold medal at last and, although in
Europe no speaker is ever asked to rise at a banquet without a minimum three glasses of wine and one of brandy
to sustain him, I would not chicken-out just because the
ordeal must be faced in American style on strawberry ice-
cream and a demi-tasse of pale coffee.

I had only a vague idea of what I ought to say, but the circumstances seemed to call for something based on my mother's moral discourse; and in my pocket lay a gold-smith's touchstone—a small diamond-shaped cube of black jasper, which I was taking over as a christening-present for an infant of that name. This made a useful starting-point. "Mr. President, ladies and gentlemen," I said, "many of you use the word 'touchstone' as a metaphor for testing the value of any poem or work of art. Perhaps few of you have ever seen a real touchstone; and because poets should avoid dead metaphors, let me show you one . . ."

I held it up, and began discoursing on gold, the royal metal, the only one found in a pure state, a metaphor for truth and integrity and, because royal and real are the same word, for reality. To be paid in gold is to be paid *really:* not in promissory notes or base metal. "The testing or assaying of doubtful gold," I went on, "has given numerous words to the English language—'touchstone,' 'acid test,' and even the word *test* itself. The original noun 'test' meant the cupel in which refiners parted gold from other metals; hence the phrase 'put it to the test.'" Hence also the phrase used by the Earl of Montrose in speaking of love:

He either fears his fate too much,
  Or his deserts are small,
Who dares not *put it to the touch*
  To gain or lose it all.

Louis Untermeyer, anthologist and jeweller, nodded sagely as I made as if to scratch the edge of my medal with the touchstone. Should the golden trace now left on the jasper, I said, be subjected to the acid test—a light application of hydrofluoric acid—it would not, like baser metals, be dissolved. . . . In the Bible, pure gold means holiness: "thou shalt overlay the ark with pure gold." And, according to the *Book of Job,* nothing exceeds pure gold in value save God's holy wisdom. . . . Pure gold is of twenty-four karat fineness. Fine gold, in English usage, goes from eighteen karats upward to twenty-four. Semi-fine gold contains no less than twelve karats; but "semi-fine" is a Gallic euphemism for the term "low gold"— everything under fine-gold standard being low gold.

I warmed to my theme, talking about karats. Karats were originally carob-seeds employed by Jewish gold-smiths as weights: twenty-four of them equalling the sixth of an ounce which was the weight of the Emperor Con-stantine's *solidus,* or gold piece. But of this number only twenty represented the gold contained in the coins; the other four represented the silver or copper which hardened it—pure gold can be bent like lead—for service as practical currency. . . . In Hebrew mysticism, carobs, *alias* locust-beans or St. John's bread, are an emblem of repentance; as the parable of the Prodigal Son who was reduced to this diet shows; and the proverb "when Israel eats carobs she will turn again to the Lord"—hence John the Baptist's choice of them as a staple. Thus carob-seeds when used as measures of fineness stand for man's conscious assessment of his failure to achieve the pure gold standard of holi-ness. . . .

I pointed to the medal. "This," I said, "though doubtless fine gold, cannot be twenty-four karat, because gold is unworkable at more than twenty-two karat fineness. And even if it could be, the award of a pure gold medal for poetry would flatter the recipient unduly: no poem ever attains such karat purity. Few of us even succeed in reach-ing the fine-gold standard; a notable exception being your

Honorary President, Robert Frost. . . . But I am glad to know, by this gift, that the Society considers my work to have attained a certain karat fineness. Most poetry nowadays is silver-gilt, or gold-filled bronze, or pinchbeck. . . ."

That went over pretty well, and I was rewarded after dinner with a couple of stiff drinks in the lounge, where a procession of poets congratulated me on the Award.

But an unwillingness to accept official valuations on trust has always been my curse. And I have a sensitive touch. That night, remembering the gold sovereigns I used to jingle in my pocket as a young man before the First World War, I poised the medal on my finger tips and decided that, for its size, it hardly weighed quite what it should. . . . Closer inspection revealed a small "14 k" stamped on the edge, next to the maker's name. "Not fine gold, but at least gold," I reassured myself.

Back home in Majorca, I found that an account of the Celebrations had been copied from the *New York Herald Tribune* in our local papers. Several Palma citizens gave me their congratulations, including Don Carlos Pomar, whose jeweller's shop I visited one morning to have a signet ring enlarged. (That is another story. In Israel, last year, I had stubbed my little finger at Sodom against a block of salt which formed Lot's Wife's skirts—an accident of enormous interest to our village priest, since it authenticated Holy Scripture—and my ring no longer went over the middle joint.)

Don Carlos asked to see the famous medal. "Do not think me curious or impertinent, but in all my life I have never handled a medal that was *oro de ley*—fine gold of eighteen karats. Spain is a poor country since President Negrin sent her entire gold reserve to Moscow; but even before that, our medals had long been gilt bronze. Sad, how many indigent Army widows have tried to sell me their husbands' gold medals and crosses won on the field of battle. . . . America, however, possesses so much gold that she can afford to bury ingots by the thousand tons in underground vaults."

"My medal has a fourteen-karat stamp," I said.

"That is not, of course, *oro de ley;* but at least you have a gold medal. Please do me the favour of letting me examine it."

"With great pleasure, friend."

In due course I brought Don Carlos the medal. He sighed. "Once again a disappointment. . . ."

"How?"

"It is not gold of any sort. It is not even engraved; and the inscription has been written with an electric needle."

"But what of this fourteen-karat stamp?"

"I do not know what regulations are in force among the North Americans; but this medal is certainly not fourteen karat. . . . You disbelieve me? Then may I scratch, very lightly, the knob which secures the ribbon?"

"Certainly."

Don Carlos scratched, and handed me a magnifying glass: "You see: here is a delicate plating of gold; underneath lies perhaps bronze, perhaps silver. . . . Let us call it silver."

"Surely you are wrong?"

"Don Roberto, you have known me, and my father before me, for thirty years! We Pomars have been jewellers for at least three centuries. Is it likely that I would be wrong?"

"Most unlikely!"

"Why should I mislead you?"

"Do not suggest such a possibility!"

So I wrote to Dr. Decker, thanking him for the honour that this Society had done me, and for his great personal kindness. I much admired the gilt medal he had pinned on my lapel and, when I went to Switzerland, would spend the hundred-dollar cheque that came with it on a real-gold replica, taking care to use the original red ribbon and pin.

Next morning I thought: "This is the sort of letter one writes but does not mail." Nevertheless, recalling my eloquent speech about poetic gold, I felt that Dr. Decker should, in justice, have taken me by an arm and revealed the truth before the banquet ended.

So I sent my letter to Robert Frost, and asked him to forward it, or not, whichever he chose. Although the demon of plain speaking has always plagued Robert, as it plagues me, he might be reluctant to compromise his standing with the Society. . . . True, Dr. Decker was a gentleman, but a letter like mine would be putting both his courtesy and his sense of humour to a severe test—indeed, an acid test.

I realize now who had dictated the letter: my mother, grieved to see her son's outstanding talents symbolically slighted. Dear Mother! If it is true that the dead know everything, she must have been aware that the fine-gold Tara brooch, always flaunted proudly on her black silk bosom, came to me after her death; and that, when I asked Don Carlos to mend the pin, he discovered that the brooch was pinchbeck. . . .

Robert Frost ("gleefully" I hear) forwarded the letter; and in due course I got from Dr. Decker a stiff but gentlemanly reply. This medal, he assured me, was "real gold for me and my heirs." If, however, by some strange mis-

chance, I had been given a trial piece struck in base
metal, he would be glad to send me a real gold replace-
ment. . . .

Stricken with shame and remorse, I hurried to Palma
again. "Look here, Don Carlos," I said. "I trusted you as
I trusted your father; but it appears that an embarrassing
error has been made. The medal is gold, or so the donors
swear. Why should they tell lies? Please test it once more,
and then I will know whether I owe them an apology."

Don Carlos smiled: "It is unnecessary. I have seen as
much as I need, Don Roberto. Why not take a second
opinion? You are acquainted with Señor Cortés, I think?
Consult him!"

Señor Cortés is perhaps the most experienced and most
affluent member of the Palma Marranos—the former
Jewish goldsmiths' guild forcibly converted to Christianity at King Philip II's orders.

I approached young Cortés, whose shop stands at the
other end of the same street. He is heavily built, swarthy,
grave, formal. "Señor Cortés, will you do me a great
favour?"

"Always at your service, Señor Gravés."

"Tell me: is this object gold?"

He did not answer, nor even glance at the medal, but
clapped his hands. "Jaimito: the touchstone and the acid!"

Jaimito, his small assistant, appeared like a genie, carry-
ing the family touchstone (just like mine, though two
inches longer) and the acid bottle.

"Will you mind if I scratch the metal, Señor Gravés?"

"Do your worst, Señor Cortés!"

He filed a minute piece from the edge, took a trace
from the exposed interior with the touchstone, applied
the acid, shook his head. "I regret to inform you, Señor

Graves," he said in even tones, "that this is not gold."

I wrung his hand. "I am delighted by your assay, Señor Cortés; and under a profound obligation to you!"

He looked at me in surprise; then, after a brief, suave nod of goodbye turned to show a woman tourist some matched strings of the "Manacor Pearls" for which this island is famous. There are, of course, no pearl-beds in the Mediterranean. . . .

I wrote again to Dr. Decker, informing him that the medal had now been twice assayed, and at each test proved not to be what he and I believed it was; but that, joking aside, I should always recall with pride the occasion of its bestowal. Nor should I expect him to send me a gold substitute. Though the "14 k" referred, in fact, to the karat-fineness of the plating—a trade device which, I understood, was neither unusual nor, so far as I knew, against the Law—a medal's intrinsic value could be of no consequence to the recipient.

Dr. Decker took this very well, assuring me that he would ask the metallurgists of his University to assay the stock of metals already struck for further Prince Alexander Droutzkoy Memorial Awards, and see whether or not mine had been exceptional. That was over a year ago, and I am still waiting for his report. But I notice that the Alexander Droutzkoy Gold Medal was not awarded in 1961.

All of you know, I suppose, that in England no gold medals have been made of gold since the First World War. It's against the Law. But I got a research-team to do a brief investigation of American gold medals for me. They report that though no legal impediment to the striking of fine-gold medals exists in the United States, such awards are now rare. The Director of the Mint licences medal-makers and jewellers to buy fine gold; yet while they must submit detailed returns on the troy ounces of gold used in manufacturing their products, they need not declare how much gold went into any particular piece. American medals, therefore, range through all degrees of fine and low gold; nor is it illegal or unethical to describe gilded bronze or silver as "gold."

If medal-makers stamp their products to indicate karat-fineness, they are subject to the Federal Stamping Act of 1906, which tolerates a deficiency of no more than one half-karat. This Act also regulates the mark to be used by makers of gold-filled or rolled-gold plated medals—two similar processes, in which sheets of gold are brazed, welded, or soldered to base metal. Legally, a medal stamped "gold filled" must contain gold equal to one-twentieth or more of its total weight; a medal marked "rolled gold plate" must contain gold equalling one-twentieth or less of its total weight; and, in each case, the stamp must indicate not only the fractional proportion of gold to the base metal, but also its karat-fineness. However, the Act can be interpreted in more ways than one. Until three years ago, it was considered lawful and ethical to describe as "gold plated" any medal cast in bronze or silver which had a gold skin at least seven one-millionth of an inch thick—the result of having been dipped into an electrolytic gold-solution. Makers of such medals were glad to stamp their products "gold plated"; but rolled-gold-platers raised an outcry, charging the electroplaters with fraud. In 1957, the Federal Trade Commission, which is-sues trade practice rules for jewellers, decided that arti-cles electroplated with a gold skin of at least seven one-millionth of an inch, might be marked (if marked at all) as "gold-electroplated"; and that where the thickness was even less, they might be marked "gold-flashed" or "gold-washed." This F.T.C. decision being unenforceable by law, the dispute has never been resolved, and gold electroplaters now seldom stamp their products; or, if they do, cannot, it seems, be restrained from marking them "14 k." As Chaucer wrote: *"Hyt is not al gold that glareth."*

Variations in the gold-content of medals have, naturally, been caused by the changing price of gold. When President Roosevelt devalued the dollar, a troy ounce of fine gold went up in price from twenty dollars to its present level of thirty-five. The medal-makers passed on this 75 per cent increase to the medal-donors; and demand for high-karat awards soon weakened. Since World War Two, however, the endowment funds of most national institutions have risen more than 75 per cent in sympathy with the stock market; and fine-gold medals are no longer ruled out by economics. Nevertheless, why give fine gold when one may safely and ethically give dross? Thus, though more "gold medals" are awarded than ever before, the gilt enormously outnumber the golden; and of these, few exceed fourteen-karat fineness.

A random golden roll. The U. S. Golf Association gave Jack Nicklaus, the amateur with the lowest score in the 1960 National Open Golf Tournament, a fourteen-karat medal. Mayor Wagner collected one of the same fineness: the Amateur Athletic Union's Gold Medal Award for "the citizen of the Metropolitan area who has best served youth and athletics during the year." The National Geographic Society's Hubbard Medal, which has gone to such heroes as Peary, Shackleton, Amundsen, Lindbergh, Byrd and Hillary, runs to fourteen karat. So does the special gold medal which the American Society for the

Prevention of Cruelty to Animals conferred in 1960 on
Baker, the intrepid Space-monkey—and, posthumously,
on Baker's luckless companion Able. The National Geographic Society's Special Gold Medal, however, given to
Prince Philip in 1957 for his not-too-perilous world tour,
measures four inches across, weighs two pounds four
ounces troy, and is of twenty-two karat fineness. Presi-
dents de Gaulle of France, and Lleras of Colombia, also
Their Majesties Bhumibol Adulyadej, King of Thailand,
and Mahendra Bir Bikram Shah Deva, King of Nepal,
have all recently won the fourteen-karat Medal of New
York City reserved for kings and heads of state. The
Massachusetts Horticultural Society's George Robert
White Medal is twenty-two karat.

But the Key of the City of New York, last presented to
the Honourable Sir Hugh Stephenson, K.C.M.G., C.I.E.,
C.U.O., O.B.E., former British Consul-General at New
York, is electroplated bronze; like the American Poetry
Society's Prince Alexander Droutzkoy's Memorial Award
for Services to Poetry. And no gold medals won by the
champion skiers who risked life and limb in the Winter
Olympics at Squaw Valley were better than "gold-filled";
so a thoughtful California firm copied them in fourteen-
and eighteen-karat gold, and put the replicas on sale—for
losers as well as winners to frame, if they wished, and
hang over their drawing-room grand pianos.

The Word 'Báraka'

ADDRESS TO THE OXFORD UNIVERSITY POETRY SOCIETY.
PREVIOUSLY GIVEN IN A MODIFIED FORM TO THE AMERI-
CAN ACADEMY AND INSTITUTE OF ARTS, AS THE BLASH-
FIELD ADDRESS

The vocabulary of Islam contains an important and powerful word: *BARAKA*. It derives from a Semitic root *BRK*, present in the Biblical name *Barak* and in the Phoenician *Barka*. (The city of Barcelona is called after Hamilcar Barca, Hannibal's father.) *Barak* or *barka* or *báraka* means lightning. Since lightning is a phenomenon everywhere attributed to the gods, *báraka* means the sudden divine rapture which overcomes either a prophet or a group of fervent devotees (Dervish dancers, for example, or the primitive Christians at the Feast of Pentecost) whom it unites in a bond of love: it can therefore stand for the blessedness acquired by holy shrines and other places where the spirit of God has been plainly manifested. The word has been adopted into Spanish, and has Hebrew equivalents; but the Jews prefer to derive *báraka* from a root meaning "knee" and therefore devotion to a god whose worshippers kneel. A poem can have *báraka*, inspired by the Muse; and the Moslem *Sufis*, surprisingly enough, own to a female Muse.

This religious metaphor invites lay uses. If a family has settled down peacefully in a house of their own choosing, every room acquires a domestic, rather than an ecstatic, *báraka*, of which the children become conscious and which spells "home." *Báraka* can thus be applied to relics, keepsakes, and other assurances of blessedness.

I always avoid using a foreign word when an English equivalent can be found. But the nearest I know to *báraka* is the Elizabethan "virtue." Tyndale's translation of *Mark* has: "such virtues (i.e. acts of blessedness) as are wrought by his hands." And the Geneva Bible: "in his own virtue (i.e. holy power) Christ rose again," and a solitary instance occurs in the King James Bible: "Jesus knowing that virtue had gone out of him . . ." This sense of "virtue" as spiritual power has become obsolete beyond revival. Virtue is now a moral habit, attributed mainly to the docile and uninspired: and *vertu* is rarity from the collector's point of view: and a *virtuoso* is an expert capable of judging such rarity.

An Arab village woman will prize the dented brass cooking pot that has done service for a generation or more, as having *báraka* and producing far tastier food than the brightest spun-aluminium saucepan in the bazaar. In the United States and England, a pair of blue jeans so often washed that they have faded almost white, or a well-worn gardening jacket, can equally possess *báraka*: and a wife's failure to recognize this while spring-cleaning often causes a deal of trouble.

John Kenneth Galbraith and his fellow-economists in the United States have emphasized that the old American ideal of thrift, which implied producing durable goods and using them with affectionate care until they disintegrated—like the One-Horse Shay of the poem—no longer thrives even in the backwoods. Instead, Expendability is preached: the manufacture and consumption of goods not meant to last for more than a short season. If a new appli-

ance proves to have an uneconomically long life, it must
be replaced by a shorter-lived substitute. With care, you
may perhaps keep this year's model working for several
years; then something will snap, and nobody will offer
to repair it. That these practices keep the wheels of in-
dustry turning, and salesmen busy, cannot be denied; but
when nothing lasts long enough to become an intregral
part of a man's life, the principles of artificial obsolescence
affect his friendships, loyalties, loves and his tastes in literature and art. The American way of life has now gained
a firm foothold in Europe.

Anything made by hand has a certain glow of life.
Factory-made objects are born dead—however apt their
design, however sound their construction, and must have
life breathed into them by affectionate use. A veteran
typewriter of which you have grown fond seems to re-
ciprocate your feelings and even encourage the flow of
thought. Though at first a lifeless assemblage of parts, it
eventually comes alive. And so did an automobile in
thriftier days. As for cameras—any good photographer is
horror-struck by the loss of a camera that has grown to
be part of himself: even if he buys an identical model,
there will be a delay of anything from six months to two
years before it learns to take his own inimitable sort of
picture. Scientists cannot explain such phenomena, and
therefore dispute the facts. Let them! *Báraka* will never
be a scientific term.

Hand-made things that have been a long time in one
household eventually come under the hammer and, if they
have any rarity, pass by way of the antique dealer and
virtuoso into the hands of the rich collector. The collector
does not use them, not even the china and table silver,

but displays them, critically labelled, behind glass. Thence
they may pass to some museum where their stored-up
báraka inevitably dies, because what sustains it is the
touch of human fingers. A collector at least lets a few
friends handle his treasures; but museum visitors are for-
bidden to touch the exhibits. Nor do museums ever dis-
gorge their exhibits, unless in wartime to drunken looters
—however crammed the cellars may be with crates of
bequests which they have no room to display. The New
York Metropolitan Museum contains no less than three
Stradivarius violins: none of them kept alive by playing.
And, as a museum curator of silver once told me in a
moment of frankness: "museum silver gets the wrong sort
of tarnish."

Báraka in literature and the creative arts is of the utmost
importance. Remember that it originally meant "divine
inspiration" or "blessedness"—a quality which the most
daring intellectual experiments, or works most shrewdly
designed for the current market, cannot possess. But the
new economy, respecting a citizen's inalienable right to
buy what he wants (or thinks that he wants), lets the
question "Will it sell?" rule commercial production. Writers and artists feel obliged to watch the market, for although a Government may have trouble in disposing of
national food surpluses, yet idleness (except among the
very rich) still counts as a sin; and public opinion is opposed to the feeding of a parasitic class whose work lacks
an assured market value; and *báraka*—the quality of life in
poems, or stories, or paintings, or sculptures, or music—is
never granted to a man more concerned with selling than
with making.

Religious ecstasy and the poetic trance, if one looks at

these phenomena subjectively, are both achieved by divine inspiration; or, if looked at objectively, by self-hypnosis. Religious ecstasy is invited by prayers, music, and solemn ritual. Formalities of verse-printing invite the poetic trance: which means, for instance, that a sonnet printed as a prose paragraph will be extremely hard to read as a poem. Prose intelligence operates on one level only; poetic intelligence operates in depth, as if under narcotics, with all its five inner senses alert. I can sharpen my point by mentioning the *báraka* resident in the King James Bible which, though not poetry, is printed in verses and retains the archaic diction and speech-rhythms of its early Tudor translators. In Britain today, this ancient *báraka*, and that of a few unrestored churches and cathedrals, keeps the flickering candle of faith alight. Yet, in the name of progress, various ecclesiastical bodies are now trying to supplant the King James version with *The New English Bible*, a translation carefully purged of all *báraka*. Though this has sold in advance by the million, the verdict of the British countryside is: "We don't like this book. The old one was holier. If I had to swear an oath on this book, I wouldn't feel bound to tell the truth." "Holiness," then, is a near-equivalent of *báraka*, especially if detached from its ecclesiastical setting—as when Coleridge wrote in *Kubla Khan*:

A savage place, as *holy* and enchanted
As e'er beneath a waning moon was haunted
By woman wailing for her demon lover . . .

and again:

Weave a circle round him thrice
An close your eyes in *holy* dread . . .

But though the formalities of printing a poem invite readers to fall under its spell, poems so rarely have *bá-raka* that the eye grows suspicious and seldom succumbs. Myself, I have come to dread the sight of a new book of poems. Too often the spell vanishes after I have read a few lines, and my prose mind reasserts itself. The poem's holy circle has been broken by some extraneous element: whether experimental affectation, or Classical convention, or incoherence, or banality, or didacticism. . . . How to create and preserve the spell must remain a mystery. But one can say, at least, that the words must, as it were, grow together, entranced by the poet's personal rhythm; and that they cannot do so unless unchallengeably his own, the familiar furniture of his mind. All attempts to borrow from the alien languages of science and philosophy will be futile; they have no emotional depth.

Anglo-American poetry of, say, 1911–1929, based on Continental models and psychological theory, provides the text-books with an interesting chapter. Though not commercial in origin, the poems lacked *báraka* because their motive was critical, rather than creative. A poem seems to choose its own colouring, voice, form, gait, character, in the blind moment of inception, just as the human embryo does; these are not predeterminable elements, except perhaps in a test-tube homunculus . . . It had been decided, at any rate, that the yoke of tradition should be broken, as the French were busily breaking theirs. This made poor sense: for French has a remarkably poor vocabulary compared with English, and its severe control by the *Academie Française* tempted anti-academic writers to acts of sabotage. Of English, on the other hand, it could be said in the words of *Ecclesiasticus:*

"An ornament of gold is her yoke, and her traces a riband of pure silk." Literature in England and the United States during the first decade of this century was, on the whole, undistinguished to the point of stuffiness—the very riches of our language had scared prominent writers into establishing strict conventions and trying to introduce a Classical impersonality based on Latin practice. Nevertheless, the younger poets did not need to revolt; but only to assert their time-honoured liberties—English, because it is a two-strand language of Anglo-Saxon and Norman-French, permits unlimited rhythmic variations on scores of metrical norms. However, their difficulty lay in this: that to be idiosyncratic without loss of principle, to create a personal poetic style that could be recognized at a glance yet resist parody, demanded too many years of work, too deep a devotion to the language, and too lonely an independence of fashion. Anti-academic experimentalism was far easier. And, paradoxically, their poems have now been accepted by English Faculties in the United States and England and become the most advanced form of academicism. Just how far this tendency has gone was forced on me recently. One of my tasks as holder of the Oxford Chair of Poetry is helping to adjudicate the Newdigate Prize Poem. Twenty-seven out of thirty-one entries were based on modernist technique. Nevertheless, that these candidates chose the modernist formula, rather than the heroic couplet to which they were limited until a few years ago, confirms my feeling that it is already on the way out. The technique that young men choose for a prize poem on a set subject is not one in which they will try to write authentic and original poetry.

The present remarkable public demand for poetry keeps pace with the growing affluence of life throughout the Western world and the gradual shrinking of the work week. Never before have such efforts been made to satisfy the demand, yet never have there been fewer original poets. "This is a critical, not a poetic, age," I am told. "Inspiration is out. Contemporary poems must reflect the prevailing analytic spirit." But I am old-fashioned enough to demand *báraka*, an inspirational gift not yet extinct, which defies critical analysis.

The present economic system is based on expendability. The museum system, which supplements it, is based on what I should call "arrestation of time." The museums emphasize the hopeless distance separating the period pieces exposed behind glass from manufactured goods in current use. A similar distance separates the home vocabulary of most schoolboys and undergraduates from that of their English Literature classes. The thread connecting the two finally snapped thirty years ago. Shakespeare is now a museum exhibit, not for home reading as when I was a boy: so are Wordsworth, Tennyson and Browning. Anyone raised under these conditions faces a difficult dilemma if he tries to write poems: his home vocabulary cannot bear the full weight of thought and emotion he may want to express; yet the museum vocabulary is so little his own that borrowings from it will look artificial.

This is not a problem that has ever worried me: I was born into a bookish family, discovered English poetry for myself at the age of ten, and escaped over thirty years ago to a Spanish village untouched by modern technology— bringing with me my personal possessions and language —which has been my home ever since. If the house seems, to visiting friends, like a museum, that is their mistake: my great-grandfather's silver candlesticks and my great-great-grandfather's spoons, as well as hundred-year-old

plates and dishes, are in daily use, and the English poets
are ranked around me on book-shelves within easy reach.
I feel contemporary with Thomas Hardy, whom I knew
well, and through him with Coleridge and Keats, and
through them with Shakespeare, Marlowe, Donne, Skelton and Chaucer. Call me a living fossil, if you like.

Expendability is, of course, closely allied to the new
phenomenon of haste. Were it not for the immense increase in speed, which makes it possible to transport goods
and raw materials in a matter of hours rather than days,
we should still be bound by the economy of thrift. The
Arabic proverb is to the point here:

Háraka Háraka ma fiha báraka.
"Haste, haste, has no virtue."

I shall leave you to find your own apt instances of
báraka in art, architecture or music. . . . In poetry, it
can cast an immortal spell on the simplest combination
of words. The Greeks held a spot struck by lightning so
sacred that they built an enclosing wall around it; true
poems are equally lightning-struck and equally insulated
by their own poetic forms against encroachments of time
and fashion. . . . There is also an anti-*báraka*, springing
from wilful lovelessness. The atmosphere of houses can
be poisoned by years of hatred; the memories of childhood can be made hideous by oppression; lovely jewels
can be cursed by greed and envy. Anti-*báraka* in poetry
derives, perhaps, from a greater hatred of hypocrisy than
an active love of truth. It is critical diabolism challenging
the self-assurance of the righteous, and welcome only
when a country's leading poets, artists, architects and

musicians are ignorant formalists. The Germans call it *Unheimlichkeit:* a sinister unhomeliness.

And let us not undervalue Mother Goose's nursery rhymes, and Edward Lear's nonsense rhymes, and sea-shanties, and occasional so-called minor poems by Herrick, Goldsmith, Crabbe, Southey, Jane Taylor, Poe, Stevenson, Longfellow, Whittier, De la Mare. Though "quaint" and "homely" have become words of polite scorn, "quaintness" is a close English equivalent of this lesser *báraka*, which combines the senses of "skilfully made," "old-fashioned," and "diverting." . . . Most first volumes of verse published today are one-man shows intended for the critics, and wholly lacking in quaintness. . . . Nothing can halt this trend, if only because the publication of expendable books, and of the criticism they provoke, keeps the busy wheels turning. It is worse in the States, where too many of their authors are sponsored by Foundations which, in turn, must find an annual quota of respectable beneficiaries. . . . Is it unrealistic to hanker after an economy of thrift and the restriction of verse to a thin golden trickle?

The Poet's Paradise

ADDRESS TO THE OXFORD UNIVERSITY HUMANIST GROUP

We have narrowed our minds by a neglect of the physical senses: relying on reason, we no longer see, hear, taste, smell or feel anything like so acutely as our primitive ancestors did, or as most little children still do before their education hardens. Henry Vaughan's *The Retreat*, imitated by Wordsworth in his better known *Intimations of Immortality*, begins:

Happy those early days when I
Shin'd in my angel-infancy,
Before I understood this place
Appointed for my second race
Or taught my soul to fancy aught
But a white celestial thought,
When yet I had not walked above
A mile or two from my first love
And looking back (at that short space),
Could see a glimpse of his bright face
When on some gilded cloud or flower
My gazing soul would dwell an hour . . .

Civilized man notices a gilded cloud and, at best, mutters "cumulus" or "cirrus" or "mare's tail," speculating on the weather it portends; notices a flower and dismisses it with a casual recognition of the variety. To gaze at a wild rose or buttercup for even a minute and find illumination in the sight, would never occur to him; if only because all his senses are blunted by a persistent disregard of the ugly smells, ugly sounds, ugly sights and unpalatable tastes which the struggle for existence entails. His spirit, also, has lost touch with the ideas of mystery, grace and love that originally informed it: intellect and habit starve out imagination. How to awaken these dormant capacities is a problem seldom raised, except by mystics, who usually suggest a daunting formula of spiritual exercises designed to tame bodily lusts. Some claim to have themselves visited Paradise in a state of trance so induced, and to have found it the seat of true felicity and perfect wisdom. Here is a typical passage from Thomas Traherne's *Centuries of Meditation* (he was a contemporary of Vaughan's):

The corn was orient and immortal wheat, which never should be reaped nor ever was sown. I thought it had stood from everlasting to everlasting. The dust and stones of the street were as precious gold: the gates were at first the end of the world. The green trees when I first saw them through one of the gates transported and ravished me: their sweetness and unusual beauty made my heart to leap, and almost mad with ecstasy, they were such strange and beautiful things . . . all things abided eternally as they were in their proper places. Eternity was manifest in the light of the day and something infinite behind everything appeared, which talked with my expectation and moved my desire.

Today, the main alleviations for the stress of commercial and industrial life are organized religion, organized entertainment, drink. Organized religion may sober the spirit, but except among the more ecstatic sects, rarely

purges it. Organized entertainment distracts, but does not
illuminate, the mind. Though some poems, melodies,
works of art, love-affairs and fever dreams may give
glimpses of a lost magical reality, their spell is short-
lasting: it does not create such a permanent nostalgia for
the fairyland of childhood as possessed, say, John Clare in
Northampton Asylum. The hard, dirty, loveless, synthetic
world re-asserts itself as the sole factual truth. Yet a
superstitious dream that, somehow, happiness, love, glory,
magic lie hidden close at hand, protects the world from
the nervous breakdown of which recent wars have been
symptomatic: a dream that, when fostered by films and
family magazines, becomes optimistically attached to personal success in a career or in marriage and, when fostered
by the Church, optimistically attached to a Paradisal aft-
erworld.

In ancient times, "Paradise" was strictly reserved for
an illuminated aristocracy, until the Church at last threw
open the gates to all converts, however brutish or feeble-
minded, who would accept baptism. Priests then preached
Heaven's glories (attainable only by a belief in Christ)
as the reward of patience and humility after traversing
this vale of tears. Yet St. John's Apocalyptic Paradise is
borrowed from chapters of the pre-Christian *Book of
Enoch*, which are themselves based on the "Eden" chapters of *Ezekiel* and *Genesis;* and these, again, on the Babylonian Paradise described in the Gilgamesh Epic and elsewhere. The Persians knew a similar Paradise; and their
name for it; *paridaeza*, yields the Syrian-Greek word
paradeisos and the Hebrew *pardess*. Those middle-East-
ern Paradises, so far back as the Sumerian, are reported as
being delightful mountain-top gardens watered by a four-
headed crystal river, their fruit-trees laden with flashing

jewels; and a wise serpent always haunts them. Rare humans who enter Paradise while in a state of grace are granted "perfect wisdom" by the Serpent—"knowledge of good and evil" means knowledge of "all things that exist"—and only the herb of immortality is denied them. Thus Gilgamesh, having visited the jewelled Babylonian Paradise, dived to the sea-bottom and drew up a herb of immortality; but the Serpent took it from him, and he meekly resigned himself to death. Adam and Eve were driven out of Eden ("pleasure") by God lest they might discover and eat the fruit of immortality; the Cherub, on guard at the gate thereafter with a flaming sword, is the very Serpent who gave them the fruit of knowledge. The King of Tyre, though perfect in beauty and wisdom, is figuratively expelled from Eden (*Ezekiel* xxviii) for claiming to be an immortal god with a seat in the heart of the sea. *Enoch* mentions both the tree of wisdom and the tree of life; and *the Secrets of Enoch* places the latter in the Third Heaven, a paradise to which St. Paul claimed that he had been caught up.

Greek mythographers told of a Paradise on Mount Atlas, the "Garden of the Hesperides," guarded by a hundred-headed Serpent; but made Heracles shoot the Serpent, take away some of the jewelled fruit, and become immortal. This Paradise, like the Sumerian one that antedates Gilgamesh's "Garden of Delights," belonged to a Mother-goddess—it was Hera's before she married Zeus—not to a male god. Christians chose to identify the Serpent in Eden with Satan; they preached that Jesus Christ, a "Second Adam," lives permanently in Paradise, having expelled the Serpent, and is ready there to welcome all believers when it has finally been destroyed on the Day of Judgment.

Why do paradises follow a traditional pattern, wide-spread and persistent enough to be shared even by Polynesians and pre-Columbian Mexicans? The evidence suggests that, originally, a common drug causes the paradisal visions and provides the remarkable mental illumination described as "perfect wisdom." One such drug, a hallucigenic mushroom, was certainly used in Central America before the Spanish conquest. Professor Roger Heim and R. G. Wasson's massive work, *Les Champignons Hallucigenes de Mexique* (Paris, 1958), contains a coloured reproduction of a fresco from the Aztec city of Tepantitla, dated between 300 and 600 A.D., which shows a soul visiting Paradise. The usual elements are there: a river (stocked with fish), bordered with flowers and bejewelled trees, haunted by bright-coloured butterflies and a spectacular serpent. The soul stands open-mouthed, weeping tears of joy and wonder, his body connected to the river by a blue thread. This river is shaped like a mushroom and, at its source—the centre of the mushroom head—lurks Tlalóc, God of Mysteries, in toad form, the water issuing from his mouth. Tlalóc, who often wore a serpent head-dress, was a god of lightning. He used a sea-shell as another emblem, and "had his seat in the midst of the seas": at the bottom of the fresco an underwater grotto appears, marked with a cross, the four heads of which are mushrooms. Nobody who has been admitted to the rite thus pictured will find much difficulty in deciphering the symbolism.

R. G. Wasson's ritual experience came as the culmination of a study on which he and his wife had been engaged for years: that of mycophobia. Mycophobia, the unreasoning fear of mushrooms, affects whole populations in Europe, Asia and Africa, being total in some regions, in others modified by certain exceptions (such as the white field mushroom among the English), elsewhere non-existent. Now, a few mushrooms, easily distinguished from edible varieties, do contain a mortal poison; but most are palatable, if not delicious. Why, the Wassons asked, when wholesome fruit and vegetables are eaten freely, with a disregard for the poisonous or the inedible, should this selectivity be denied the mushroom? Why should horrible and obscene names be applied to edible mushrooms? Perhaps mycophobia pointed to an ancient taboo, like that which has given Jews and Moslems a disgust of pork, and Northern Europeans a disgust of horse-flesh—nutritious and tasty meat—both pig and horse having once been holy animals. And, since mushrooms figured alongside toads, snakes and devils in numerous late mediaeval paintings, and still bear popular names connected with toads, snakes and devils, it looked as if they might have been sacred food in a pagan rite, preserved by witches of Western Europe who kept toads and snakes as diabolic "familiars."

A particular variety of mushroom, the *amanita muscaria*, in Britain called "fly-cap," grows under birch-trees in Northern countries, where it is scarlet with white spots; but under conifers to the southward, where its scarlet becomes fox-colour. Fly-cap induces in the Korjaks, a Palaeo-Siberian tribe of Kamchatka, and among the Mongol Hazaras of Afghanistan, a boisterous ecstasy which helps them to consult ancestral spirits and utter prophecies. R. G. Wasson guessed that the mushroom had been similarly used in Europe, though reserved for the priesthood; that, for security reasons the taboo had been extended to cover the eating of all mushrooms, on pain of death; and that this taboo hung on long after

the rites came to an end—except in countries where
famine forced the common people to defy it and become
positive mycophiles, as all Slavonic peoples now are. The
name "toadstool," particularly applied to fly-cap, is apt;
because it contains a poison, *bufotenine,* which is also
exuded by toads from their "warts" when frightened.

Moreover, early Spanish archives mentioned Mexican
mushroom-oracles that, though officially extinct, were
still rumoured to operate in secret far from civilization.
A certain mushroom was known as "God's Body" by the
Mazateks of Oaxaca Province, because sacramentally
eaten. The Wassons, learning of this, visited Oaxaca
during the June mushroom season, and were able to
attend an oracular meeting at which the *curandero*
("healer") who took charge, ceremoniously ate certain
small ill-tasting mushrooms and, speaking for the god,
gave an unexpected, surprising and accurate answer to
the question they had asked him. Later, when invited by
a *curandera* to eat the mushrooms themselves, they understood the solemn local tradition about the feast: "One
knows all; one even sees where God dwells." Their
visions recalled the heaven shown on the Tepantitla fresco,
and it became clear that they had been symbolically
eating the body not of Christ, but of the god Tlalóc.

In the different regions of Mexico where the cult survives, certain religious rules are common to all. Devotees,
before partaking of a mushroom feast, must fast, abstain
from sexual intercourse, and be at peace with the world
and themselves. Whoever disregards these rules (the
curanderos and *curanderas* agreed) may see such demonic
visions as to wish they had never been born. The Christian, Jewish, Greek and Babylonian Heavens, it should be
recalled, have a Hell which complements Paradise; and

the usual vision is of innumerable demon faces grinning from lurid caverns. But those who attend such a feast while in a state of grace, report that the mushrooms not only sharpen their intelligence, so that they seem to possess "perfect wisdom," but shower on them what Christians call "the peace and love that passes all understanding" —a strong, non-erotic sense of spiritual comradeship.

The Roman Catholic Church teaches that Paradise cannot be attained except by repentance; and prepares every sinner for the journey with the *viaticum*, a symbolic consumption of Jesus Christ's body and blood, after asking him to purge his soul by a sincere confession. From what religion, it should be asked, did St. Paul borrow this rite, since it is not attested in the Gospels and is an infringement of the Hebrew law against the drinking of blood? A question that leads to another: in what pre-Christian cult did a god deliver oracles when his flesh was symbolically eaten—as the Mazateks now believe that Tlalóc-Christ does? Tlalóc, we know, was the spirit of lightning-engendered toadstools. More questions arise. What European god claimed this nativity? Or had associations with the serpent or the toad? Or possessed an underwater retreat? Or assisted at mysteries where ineffable visions were witnessed?

The sole European deity known to have matched Tlalóc in these respects was Dionysus. Born as a serpent-crowned child from the Earth-goddess Semele, whom a flash of lightning had impregnated, he went through a variety of transformations, was then torn to shreds and eaten by the Titans, but restored to life by his grandmother, the Goddess Rhea, Creatrix of the world; possessed an underwater retreat in the grottoes of the Sea-goddess Thetis; and assisted at the chief Greek Mysteries, under the protection of goddesses.

The Greek poets tell how when Dionysus' Maenads tore off Orpheus' head, it continued to prophesy. The head of Pentheus, another figure in the Dionysus myth, was torn off by his own mother Agave; both incidents could refer to the practice of tearing the mushroom-head from its stalk—heads alone are used at Mexican oracles. The Eleusinian Mysteries, sacred to the goddesses Demeter and Persephone, and also to Dionysus, were preceded by fasting and a ritual bath in the sea, where devotees transferred their sins to scape-pigs. They then entered a temple, drank mint-water and ate pastries baked in magical shapes and carried in baskets. As a result, they saw celestial visions which could never afterwards be forgotten. The meaning of the Greek word *mysterion* ("mystery") is disputed, but since the mysteries were an autumnal festival complementary to the spring *anthesterion*, and since this means "flower-springing," *mysterion* may well mean *myko-sterion*, or "mushroom-springing."

A distinction should here be drawn between the wild Dionysian orgies of Maenads who went raging over the hills, often in the company of Satyrs (a pre-Hellenic mountain tribe), and the decently conducted temple-mysteries, where no violence occurred. Pliny's remark that an awed hush "descends on people if a toad is placed among them" suggests that Dionysus, like Tlalóc, had a toad epiphany. But the celestial visions of the mysteries are unlikely to have been produced by fly-cap, which loses its toxic quality when cooked, and could not well be introduced raw into food and drink. However, the toxic qualities of *panaeolus papilionaceus*, a hallucigenic toadstool shown on an early Greek vase and now known to have figured in the European witch cult, resist cooking; its liquor may have been mixed in the mint-water, and its flesh baked in the magical pastries. I believe, but cannot prove, that fly-cap, which appears on a carved Etruscan mirror at the feet of the criminal Ixion, was the original mushroom sacred to the universal Toad-god, and that the more tranquil and equally delightful properties of *panaeolus papilionaceus* and *psilocybe*, were discovered by later experiment and also placed under the Toad-god's charge. Fly-cap grows in both hemispheres, and the ancient mushroom-stones of Guatemala show Tlalóc in toad shape, seated underneath a mushroom which appears to be a fly-cap, not a *psilocybe*.

Some of the Eleusinian pastries had phallic shapes and, indeed, *mykes* ("mushroom") also means "phallus" in Greek; others were baked like piglings (a widespread term for mushrooms); some perhaps like toads and serpents. A common name for the toad in European folklore is "the cripple," because of his clumsy feet; and "Dionysus" means "the lame god." One Greek hero who, according to the myths, at first resisted Dionysus, but presently saw the light, was Perseus, King of Argos and founder of Mycenae. Punished for his obduracy with an outbreak of madness among the Argive women—they began eating their own babies raw, as also happened at Thebes when Pentheus resisted the cult—Perseus dedicated a temple to Dionysus at Mycenae. Argos had a toad as its badge, and Perseus is said to have named Mycenae after a mushroom found on the site, "from which proceeded a stream of water." He also made visionary flights through the air, paid a visit to the "Stygian nymphs" on the slopes of Mount Atlas—presumably the Hesperides, who were later kind to his descendant Heracles—and claimed the same sort of nativity as Dionysus, having been engendered by Zeus in a shower of gold. Phryneus, the Toadstool-Dionysus to which these myths point, lay securely hidden behind the Wine-Dionysus and the Grain-Dionysus. Apart from a menacing Greek proverb "Mushrooms are the food of the gods," nobody mentioned the subject. Greek peasants are mycophobes.

Baby-eating, a practice not associated with any Greek cult except that of Dionysus, also figured (according to Catholic missionaries) in the Aztec rain-making rites of Tlalóc. This god's name meant "Pulp of the Earth" (i.e. mushroom?), and he lived at Tlalócan, a mountain paradise, with certain Grain-goddesses and his gentle sister-spouse Chalchiuthlicue, patroness of streams and family-life. Some centuries before the Spanish conquest, matriarchy and clan-totemism had been superseded among the Aztecs by patriarchy and individual totemism. Tlalóc thus officially escaped from the tutelage of goddesses, just as Dionysus did in Classical Greece when he was raised to the Olympic Council of Twelve and took over the Barley-goddess Demeter's winnowing festival, the Haloa. Yet in the Mysteries, Dionysus seems still to have been subservient to Demeter and Persephone. Similarly, the Mazatec *curandera* who initiated the Wassons addressed the Christianized Tlalóc as if he were her wayward son, and she a goddess. It is possible that, alike in Greece and Mexico, the "babies" eaten in sacred pictures were really mushrooms.

The Christian sacrament of bread and wine was a love-feast in Hellenistic style. Initiates of the Lesser Eleusinian Mysteries, who had to undergo a period of probation before being admitted to the Greater Mysteries, saw no celestial visions. Presumably, the mystagogues withheld the sacred hallucigenic agent until sure of a candidate's worthiness; he received bread and wine only, symbols of the Grain-Dionysus and the Wine-Dionysus. The Church has indeed banished the Serpent from Paradise. Her sacramental elements give the communicant no visionary foretaste of the new Jerusalem. The disappointment often felt by Protestant adolescents at their first communion is a natural one—the priest promises more than they are able to experience. I learned only last week, from an Arabic scholar, that the root-word F.T.R. means, in Arabic, first "toadstool," then "divine rapture," then "sacred pellets of bread." This points to a pre-Islamic hallucigenic practice of immense age.

Granted, many Christian mystics and Jewish mystics have undoubtedly seen Paradisal sights, but always after a life of intense spiritual struggle; and these often alternate with terrifying visions of Hell. It is now therefore usual to treat mystics as schizophrenics, arresting them and prescribing electric-shock treatment if their enthusiasm has caused a breach of the peace. The Church herself is apt to discourage a mystic who claims to have seen sights denied to his ecclesiastical superiors; suspecting him, at best, of spiritual pride. This type of schizophrenia is chronic, uncontrollable, and what is called "anti-social." Only when mystics have written poems, or painted pictures, in which the illumination cannot be denied, and only when they have been dead some years—for example St. John of the Cross, El Greco, Blake, van Gogh—are they likely to be valued as great souls.

The use of hallucigenic mushrooms, on the other hand, induces a temporary, controllable schizophrenia within the Mazatek social scheme, and the sole religious demand on participants is that they shall enter the circle fasting, with a clear conscience and a quiet mind. When I ate

psilocybe on 31 January 1960, a recording of the
curandera's invocation to Tlalóc as Christ gave the rite
a decent solemnity. *Psilocybe* must be eaten in complete
darkness—because the least light, even strained through
the eyelids, becomes painful as soon as the drug takes
effect. The visions last for some four and a half hours.
According to the Mazateks, a novice seldom sees persons
or historical scenes: he finds it enough to enter the
"Garden of Delights." The second and third feast may
widen his experiences. Adepts learn to direct their mind
wherever they please, visit the past, foretell the future.

Here is the account I wrote of my experience:

That evening, four of us gathered in Gordon Wasson's
apartment overlooking the East River, prepared to set out
for Paradise under his guidance. He had advised us to fast
beforehand, drink no liquor, and try to achieve a state of
grace. At seven-thirty he gave us the mushrooms in crystal-
line form washed down with water and, at eight, began
turning out the lights one by one, while we settled down in
easy chairs. Soon no sound was heard except the swish-
swish of cars passing in an endless stream along the Drive
between us and the river: a noise not unlike the sound of
waves on a beach.

By eight o'clock I felt a numbness in my arms, and a
pricking at the nape of my neck. In the half-light that
filtered through the shutters, coloured dots appeared on the
ceiling; they shone brighter when I closed my eyes. We all
began to shiver, our pulses slowed down, and Masha Wasson brought in blankets. Since she is a trained nurse and
had twice made this journey herself, we welcomed the re-
assuring pressure of her hand. I remembered a warning
quotation: "You are going where God dwells; and will be
granted all knowledge. . . . Whoever nurses evil in his heart
sees hideous demons and nameless horrors, more proper to
Hell than to Paradise, and wishes he had never been born."
I anxiously considered my own motives. How honest were
they? Would I see demons? Though not a saint, I was at

least a dedicated historian and poet; with luck I might be spared punishment.

Since even the half-light had become uncomfortably strong for my eyes, I kept them closed. I knew that the road to Paradise often begins under the sea, or from a lake-bottom; so the greenish water now lapping around me came as no surprise. I entered a marble grotto, passing a pile of massive sunken statuary, and found myself in a high-roofed tunnel lit by brilliantly coloured lamps. The sea lay behind.

This was a perfect schizophrenia. My corporeal self reclined in a chair, fully conscious, exchanging occasional confidences with friends: but another "I" had entered the tunnel —perhaps the same tunnel through which, four thousand years before, the epic hero Gilgamesh made his approach to the Babylonian Paradise?

Still worrying about the demons, I glanced up at the roof. Thousands of pink, green or yellow faces, like carnival masks, grimaced horribly down; but I dismissed them with a wave of my hand, and they obediently vanished. . . . A turn in the tunnel brought me to the domed Treasury, without which no Paradise is complete, whether Hindu, Babylonian, Hebrew, Icelandic, Irish, Greek or Chinese. As the prophet Ezekiel wrote:

> Every precious stone was thy covering: the sardius, topaz, and the diamond; the beryl, the onyx and the jasper; the sapphire, the emerald, the carbuncle and gold.

Her Majesty's Crown Jewels at the Tower of London would have looked tawdry by comparison with the fantastic treasure now heaped before me: diadems, tiaras, necklaces, crosses, breast-plates, goblets, ephods, cups, platters, sceptres, blazing or twinkling. But, even richer than these jewels, were the royal silks spread out for my inspection in blue, mulberry and white: vast lengths, miraculously brocaded with birds, beasts, flowers. . . . My closest experience to this had been in early childhood when, after waiting endlessly in the cold, dark hall, my sisters and I saw the drawing-room door suddenly flung open, and there blazed the Christmas tree: all its candles lighted, its branches glistening with many-coloured tinsel.

I reached for a notebook and wrote: "9 P.M. Visions of
. . ." but got no further: things were happening too fast.
Besides, the pen felt strange in my hand, and its scratch on
paper sounded offensively loud. I remember saying after
awhile: "I have seen enough treasure for a lifetime. Is there
no human beauty in Paradise?" At once the diadems, tiaras,
necklaces, crosses and sceptres vanished, as the demons had
done. Instead, a row of lovely, live, naked Caryatids appeared, lined along the wall, as if supporting the dome. Their
faces were shrouded. Yet I hesitated to indulge in erotic
fancies, lest the Caryatids turned into filthy, deformed devil-
kins like the ones in Flemish pictures of St. Anthony's
Temptations. Blushing, I dismissed them too, and came out
from the tunnel into daylight. What I had been taught at
school and in church proved true enough, though the truth
enormously transcended the account. Around me lay a mountain-top Eden, with its jewel-bright trees, its flowers and its
pellucid streams. And I experienced not only the bliss of
innocence, but also the "knowledge of good and evil." Most Christians understand this phrase as meaning the power to distinguish
right from wrong; in Hebrew, however, it signifies a universal
understanding of all things, whether good or evil. Indeed, my
mind suddenly became so agile and unfettered that I felt capable
of solving any problem in the world; it was as if I had immediate
access to all knowledge everywhere. But the sensation of wisdom
sufficed—why should I trouble to exploit it?

Gordon Wasson had switched on the tape-recorder and
the *curandera's* voice was now invoking Tlalóc as "Christo."
She chanted, scolded, entreated, commanded, coaxed him
to do what she required; it might have been the Goddess
Aphrodite addressing her froward son Eros. . . . Every now
and then she would change her mood and song; would
mourn, triumph, or laugh. I fell wholly under her spell,
and presently enjoyed the curious experience of *seeing* sound.
The song-notes became intricate links of a round golden
chain that coiled and looped in serpentine fashion among
jade-green bushes: the only serpent I met in Eden. . . .
Each song was followed by a pause, and always I waited in
a lover's agony for her to begin again, tears pricking at my
eyelids. Once the *curandera* seemed to sing off-key. Perhaps
this was quarter-tone music; at any rate, my ear was not

offended: I knew what she meant when I saw one edge of the golden chain band now formed by the sound spread out into a spectrum; and laughed for pleasure. Towards the end came a quick, breathless, cheerful song of creation and growth. The notes fell to earth but rose once more in green shoots which soared swiftly up, putting on branches, leaves, flowers—until it dominated the sky like the beanstalk in the fairytale.

My spirit followed after into the clear blue air, gazing down on cornfields, fields of poppies, and the spires of a heavenly city, and Thomas Traherne's orient and immortal wheat, "which never should be reaped nor ever was sown."

At last the music ended. The visions were fading now. My corporeal self sighed, stretched luxuriously, and looked around. Most of the company had left the room. Only one friend remained. I asked him: "So the journey seems to be over?"

"Ah, but close your eyes, and you can get back at once," he said.

"How do you feel?"

"My mind has never been so clear! Did you hear such music in all your life?"

We joined the others in the kitchen, ate cold turkey sandwiches and compared notes. . . . "I saw huge slow-moving fish in the sea; did you?"—". . . The demons scared me nearly to death! I wept and sobbed; maybe I wasn't in a state of grace. And when I looked at my hand, O God!"—". . . Weren't those buildings *enormous?* But I couldn't place their architectural style."—". . . Me, I'd take the journey all over again—this minute, if I could!"

A curious bond of affection had been established between us: so strong that I felt nothing could ever break it. At two o'clock in the morning we said good-bye. By eight I was on my way to Idlewild, headed for Europe: profoundly refreshed, and (in Wordsworth's phrase) "trailing clouds of glory"—wisps of celestial memory which persisted nearly a month.

Civilized consciences revolt against the abuse of hallucigenic drugs—most of them habit-forming, dangerous, and unobtainable except by prescription, or in the black market. Spirits, tobacco, tranquillizers—all harmful if habitually taken—are however on unrestricted sale and, because they provide no visions (apart from the fearful hell of *delirium tremens*), the Churches condone their use; for hard liquor merely depresses the senses, tobacco and tranquillizers merely dull them.

Psilocybin, the active principle of *psilocybe*, is now synthetically made in Switzerland. At present, the medical profession controls the supply, and uses it for the diagnosis of mental illness. But, since the formula has been published, not even severe legislation will prevent the general public from access to the product. It seems likely, therefore, that what was for thousands of years a sacred and secret element, entrusted only to persons chosen for their good conduct and integrity, will soon be snatched at by jaded sensation-seekers. They will be disappointed. The word "drug," originally applied to all ingredients used in chemistry, pharmacy, dyeing and so on, has acquired a particular connotation in modern English, which cannot apply to *psilocybin:* "to drug" is to stupefy, rather than to quicken, the senses. *Psilocybin* provides no welcome semi-death in drunken stupor: though the body is relaxed, the mind is conscious throughout, indeed, supra-conscious. Psychiatrists at the Lexington Addiction Centre, Kentucky, who give *psilocybin* to alcoholics as a means of discovering why they are trying to escape from reality by drink, find that it intensifies and lays bare mental conflict. Experimentalists are therefore likely to see visions evoked by their own uneasy consciences: weeping for grief, not joy; or even shuddering aghast.

Good and evil alternate in most people's hearts. Few are habitually at peace with themselves; and whoever prepares to eat hallucigenic mushroom should take as careful stock of his mental and moral well-being as initiates took before attending the Eleusinian Mysteries. The friend who ate mushrooms with us while not in a state of peace watched his hand turn corpse-like and slowly disintegrate into a dusty skeleton. This peculiar virtue of *psilocybin*, the power to enhance personal reality, turns "Know thyself!" into a practical precept; and may commend it as the sacramental food of some new religion. *Peyotl*, made from cactus buds, another sacred hallucigenic agent—but, it seems, not in such early religious use among the Mexicans as mushrooms—has already been sanctified by a "Christian church" of two hundred thousand members, extending from Central America to Canada. The Catholic and main Protestant churches can never of course, accept visions that either *peyotl* or *psilocybin* excites as anything but diabolical and illusory. They may even put pressure on public-health authorities to outlaw *psilocybin*, arguing that, although the *psilocybe* mushroom does not make for addiction among the Mazateks, and seems to have no harmful effect on their minds and bodies, this may be due to its short season and a loss of virtue when dried; whereas the virtue is stable in *psilocybin*, and the results of long-term dosing are unknown— a permanent schizophrenia might occur. Liquor and tobacco interests would, no doubt, wholeheartedly support the Churches' plea.

My single experience of *psilocybe* was wholly good: an illumination of the mind, a re-education of sight and hearing, and even of touch, as I handled small objects beside me. The perfect sensory control which I could enjoy, confirmed, by analogy, my lifelong faith in the poetic trance: a world where words come to life and combine, under the poet's supra-conscious guidance, into inevitable and true rhythmic statements. But I find one main difference between the two conditions: a mushroom trance is relatively passive; a poetic trance, active—the pen running briskly across paper.

Research should show how far the similarity of most people's visits to Eden or Tlalócan depends on the mushrooms' toxic properties, and how far on suggestion. I think it unnecessary, here, to cite Jung's theory of the Collective Unconscious, since a common tradition of Paradise may be attributed to ancient cultural contact even between distant civilizations, especially if these experiences can be shown to correspond with the physical action of a common toxin. A distinct lowering of body-temperature occurs an hour after eating *psilocybe,* which would explain both the cool sea-grottoes and Gilgamesh's search for the herb of immortality at the sea bottom; it is also followed by a considerable heightening of colour sensitivity, which would account for the jewels. After all, such writhing and creeping things as torment sufferers from *delirium tremens* are clearly not products of the Collective Unconscious, but due to a characteristic tremor of the optic nerve and an irritation of the skin, caused by alcohol.

Paradise, in fact, seems to be a subjective vision. As Jesus himself said: "The Kingdom of Heaven is within you." He might have added: "So is the Kingdom of Hell." The jewelled "Garden" can be attained by the pure of heart without undergoing so austere a regimen as to become alienated from their friends; many young women have a secret garden which they frequently visit. The love-feast, for all who attend it in a state of grace and with complete mutual trust—by no means a simple condition—strengthens human friendship and at the same time bestows spiritual enlightenment: which are the twin purposes of most religions. Whether the soul visits a non-subjective Paradise or Hell on quitting its body, let theologians dispute.

The natural poetic trance, however, as I have experienced it on different levels—sometimes light, sometimes so deep that the slightest disturbance causes acute distress —means a good deal more to me than any trance induced by artificial means. I understand Coleridge's depreciation of *Kubla Khan*, which he wrote almost automatically after stupefying his mind with laudanum. It was, as it were, a demon's gift; not earned (like his other poems) by active poetic thought. True, I have survived enough operations to know the difference in kind between an opiate dream, where one is the dazed victim, and a mush-room vision that can, I know, be consciously assessed and even controlled. Since I found myself capable of dismissing that vision of Crown Jewels and Caryatids, and since one or two of my companions found it possible to visit par-ticular places when under the influence of *psilocybe*, I hesitate to challenge the claim that Tlalóc's adepts can use their liberation of mental forces for oracular research. Nevertheless, it seems established that Tlalócan, for all its sensory marvels, contains no palace of words presided over by the Living Muse, and no small white-washed cell (furnished with only a table, a chair, pen, ink and paper) to which a poet may retire and actively write poems in her honour—rather than bask sensuously under her spell.